THE COMPLETE GUIDE TO

ANTI-INFLAMMATORY FOODS

© 2021 Quarto Publishing plc

This edition published in 2021 by Chartwell Books,
an imprint of The Quarto Group
142 West 36th Street, 4th Floor, New York, NY 10018 USA
T (212) 779-4972, F (212) 779-6058
www.QuartoKnows.com

Chartwell titles are also available at discount for retail, wholesale, promotional, and bulk purchase. For details, contact the Special Sales Manager by email at specialsales@quarto.com or by mail at The Quarto Group, Attn: Special Sales Manager, 100 Cummings Center Suite 265D, Beverly, MA 01915 USA

ISBN: 978-0-7858-3959-0

Conceived, designed, and produced by
The Bright Press, an imprint of The Quarto Group
The Old Brewery, 6 Blundell Street,
London N7 9BH, United Kingdom
T (0) 20 7700 6700
www.QuartoKnows.com

Publisher: James Evans
Editorial Director: Isheeta Mustafi
Managing Editor: Jacqui Sayers
Project Editor: Anna Southgate
Art Director: James Lawrence
Designer: Studio Noel
Picture Research: Studio Noel
Reviewed by Katie Chapmon, MS, RD
Editorial Assistant: Chloë Porter
Cover image from Dreamstime: Victoria Shibut.
Back cover images from Shutterstock; back left: natalia bulatova;
back center: New Africa; back right: Marian Weyo

Manufactured in Singapore

10 9 8 7 6 5 4 3 2

While every care has been taken in presenting this material, the information is not intended to replace professional nutritional advice; it should not be used as a guide for self-treatment or self-diagnosis. Neither the author nor the publisher may be held responsible for any type of damage or harm caused by the use or misuse of information in this book and any person with a condition requiring medical attention should consult a qualified medical practitioner or therapist.

THE COMPLETE GUIDE TO

ANTI-INFLAMMATORY FOODS

TO SUPPORT YOUR HEALTH AND IMMUNE SYSTEM

Lizzie Streit, MS, RDN, LD

chartwell
books

[CONTENTS]

[INTRODUCTION]

Welcome to your guide to anti-inflammatory foods! The information, tips, and recipes on the following pages are tools that you can use to combat inflammation in the body through diet. Whether you picked up this book to help manage a chronic condition or just purchased it out of curiosity, the contents are helpful for everyone—beginner cooks and nutrition aficionados alike.

Chronic inflammation is comparable to a fire in your body—one that can be stoked by certain foods, lack of sleep, and stress—that gets bigger over time. And just like a fire, the damage can be lasting and widespread. Many diseases, including heart disease, type 2 diabetes, arthritis, depression, and digestive issues, are associated with chronic inflammation.

Fortunately, antioxidant-rich fruits and vegetables, healthy fats, and high-fiber foods may help "put out" this fire. And that's where this book comes into play. Its 50 featured foods all have anti-inflammatory properties. When added to your diet, especially in place of pro-inflammatory foods, they can help soothe chronic inflammation and improve health.

If changing your diet is new and intimidating to you, don't fret. You'll learn tips and tricks for choosing and cooking these foods to maximize their benefits. Each section showcases easy ways to eat more of that food, including affordable and approachable options.

Ready to get started on your delicious journey to beating inflammation? Let's dive in!

Leafy greens (above), berries, and cherries (opposite) are all rich in antioxidants—compounds that help to support anti-inflammatory processes in the body.

[HOW TO USE THIS BOOK]

Beginning with an overview of chronic inflammation, the opening sections of this book discuss the foods and lifestyle choices that increase inflammation as well as the guidelines for anti-inflammatory eating. Next, you'll find a directory of 50 of the best inflammation-fighting foods and delicious recipes that incorporate them.

The foods included in this book were chosen based on the following criteria:

- Each food is a rich source of anti-inflammatory nutrients or compounds.
- There is growing research to back the food's anti-inflammatory potential.
- Foods from every food group are included, to ensure that the reader has a variety of choices for putting together meals.

While all of the foods in this book contain many nutrients and compounds that may have anti-inflammatory potential, only some of their mechanisms are highlighted. Most of what is known about these foods is based on test-tube and animal studies, in addition to some observational studies and clinical trials. The research on this topic is still fairly limited, and more extensive research and large-scale human trials are needed to fully understand the role of food in chronic inflammation. Only 50 of the most well-known anti-inflammatory foods are included, but there are numerous other foods that have inflammation-fighting properties.

No one food is considered a cause or cure for chronic inflammation. Instead, it's thought that eating a variety of foods with certain nutrients, such as antioxidants, omega-3 fatty acids, and fiber, supports anti-inflammatory processes in the body. This can help in the management or prevention of conditions related to chronic inflammation, but it's not a guaranteed cure.

WHOLE FOODS VS. SUPPLEMENTS

Do supplement forms of compounds found in anti-inflammatory foods work as well as eating the whole foods themselves? Maybe, but it's more likely that a number of compounds work synergistically to fight inflammation. Therefore, it is usually better, and safer, to eat foods with anti-inflammatory properties than to take supplements containing one or two isolated compounds.

Salmon is a good source of omega-3 fatty acids, which are known for calming inflammation.

Introduction: An overview of the food type with a brief outline of its anti-inflammatory potential.

Nutrition Box: Lists the basic nutritional values of each food.

Your Diet: Discusses the pros and cons of the food type in relation to special diets.

How to Eat More: Suggests ways to incorporate more of the food type as snacks or in recipes.

Did You Know?: Offers a lesser-known fact or a myth-buster about each type.

For each of the 50 foods in the following chapter, you'll learn about:

- Its anti-inflammatory effects
- What to look for when selecting the food
- Maximizing anti-inflammatory potential during cooking
- Ways to eat more of it
- How the food fits into a range of special diets and considerations for those with medical conditions

You can read this book from start to finish or flip to a food of interest to learn more about it. If you are not familiar with anti-inflammatory eating, it will be helpful to read the beginning sections before moving onto the foods. On the following pages, you will find a glossary of the most common terms used in association with anti-inflammatory foods.

If you have questions or concerns about incorporating foods, take medications that may interact with foods, or have a medical condition that requires a special diet, consult with your health care provider before making changes to your diet based on this book.

GLOSSARY OF TERMS

Throughout this book, you will encounter scientific terms related to inflammation and anti-inflammatory properties. Here is a list of these terms and their definitions to refer to as you read.

Antioxidants: Molecules that protect cells from free radical damage; there are likely thousands of substances that act as antioxidants, including vitamins C and E, beta-carotene, carotenoids, flavonoids, selenium, and many more.

Carotenoids: Pigments that give plants yellow, orange, and red colors and promote health, including beta-carotene, lutein, and lycopene.

Flavonoids: A large subfamily of polyphenols, including flavanols, catechins, resveratrol, anthocyanins, quercetin, kaempferol, apigenin, and isoflavones.

Free radicals: Reactive molecules that are natural byproducts of digesting food, exercise, and inflammation but can also form after exposure to cigarette smoke, ultraviolet rays, pollutants, certain drugs, and other environmental factors.

Glycemic index (GI): A scale used to assess the ability of a certain food to raise blood sugar levels. A high GI food causes rapid increases in blood sugar.

Gut microbiome: Also known as gut flora or microbiota and it refers to the bacteria and microorganisms in the digestive tract. Beneficial bacteria are known as probiotics and are fed by prebiotics.

Inflammatory markers: Blood can be tested for specific markers that indicate the presence of inflammation in the body. The tests analyze levels of C-reactive protein (CRP) in the blood, and pro-inflammatory cytokines such as tumor necrosis factor-alpha (TNF-alpha) and interleukin-6 (IL-6).

Carrots get their vibrant orange coloring from the carotenoid beta-carotene.

Omega-3 fatty acids: Polyunsaturated fatty acids that fight inflammation, including alpha-linolenic acid (ALA), found in plant foods, and eicosapentaenoic acid (EPA) and docosahexaenoic acid (DHA), mainly found in fish.

Oxidative stress: A state of imbalance between free radical production and antioxidant levels in the body. It's also referred to as oxidative damage. In this state, free radicals can harm cells, leading to inflammation, which in turn contributes to inflammatory diseases.

Polyphenols and phenolic compounds: A large family of beneficial plant compounds that are thought to offer anti-inflammatory and antioxidant effects.

[WHAT IS INFLAMMATION?]

Inflammation is part of the body's response to injury or infection. The familiar signs and symptoms of acute inflammation—swelling, redness, and pain—are normal and healthy. But when inflammation persists over time, it becomes problematic. Unlike acute inflammatory processes that get kickstarted after an infection, cut, or injury, chronic inflammation has subtler symptoms and persists for much longer.

Low-grade, chronic inflammation causes the body and immune system to remain on high alert. It typically has no overt signs, but can be marked by symptoms such as joint and body pain, fatigue, depression and anxiety, and constipation, diarrhea, or other digestive issues. Some of the root causes of chronic inflammation include poor diet, stress, lack of physical activity, poor sleep, smoking, excess alcohol intake, and obesity.

INFLAMMATORY DISEASES

Over time, chronic inflammation wreaks havoc on the body, damages cells, and contributes to risk factors that precede many diseases and ailments. Here are some of the conditions associated with chronic inflammation:

- Heart disease
- Hypertension
- Heart attack or stroke
- Cancer
- Type 2 diabetes
- Alzheimer's disease and other dementias
- Depression and anxiety
- Psoriasis
- Lupus
- Rheumatoid arthritis
- Inflammatory bowel disease (Crohn's and colitis)
- Fatty liver disease
- Kidney disease
- Asthma

Please note that inflammation has not been identified as the sole cause of these conditions but may contribute to their development.

Regular exercise can combine with a healthy diet to reduce inflammatory markers.

DIET AND INFLAMMATION

Poor diet is thought to be a major contributor to chronic inflammation. Certain foods promote inflammation through a variety of mechanisms. Saturated and trans fats, alcohol, and refined sugars and carbohydrates may increase the release of inflammatory messengers or alter gut bacteria and intestinal lining in ways that promote inflammation. These foods also contribute to oxidative stress, a state of imbalance between free radicals that damage cells and the antioxidants that scavenge them. The factors outlined on the following page offer an overview of the main interactions between diet and inflammation.

Tomatoes, walnuts, parsley, and yogurt are all high-ranking anti-inflammatory foods.

BLOOD SUGAR

Diets that are high in added sugars and refined carbohydrates, such as pastries, desserts, candy, sodas, and foods made with white flour, can contribute to insulin resistance and high blood sugar levels. Insulin is the hormone that's released after the consumption of carbohydrates. It promotes the uptake of glucose (sugar) from the blood into the cells. During insulin resistance, cells become less efficient at maintaining healthy blood sugar levels. Over time, high blood sugar levels contribute to oxidative stress and trigger the release of inflammatory compounds. This phenomenon is particularly evident in individuals with type 2 diabetes. Natural sugars, such as those from fruit, and complex carbohydrates, like whole grains and starchy vegetables, do not have the same impact on insulin and blood sugar.

Breads made whole grains are better for your digestive system, while yogurt (opposite) is one of the best sources of probiotics.

GUT HEALTH

Too many refined carbohydrates and sugars, highly processed foods, alcohol, and saturated or trans fats may harm the lining of the gut and make it more permeable. Eating a lot of these foods, while not getting enough fiber, also seems to disrupt the gut microbiome. When gut lining is compromised, irritants can "leak" from the gut into the rest of the body and cause inflammation. Plus, imbalances in gut bacteria can trigger inflammatory processes. Eating foods that contain probiotics ("good" bacteria) and prebiotics (dietary fibers that "feed" probiotics) promotes a healthy microbiome.

OBESITY

Excess body weight may contribute to inflammation. Fat tissue is thought to release pro-inflammatory cytokines, including IL-6 and TNF-alpha. Chronic inflammation is part of the reason why obesity is a risk factor for heart disease, type 2 diabetes, and increased risk of infection. Eating a diet rich in plant foods, healthy fats, and lean proteins can help you maintain a healthy weight.

A beet and buckwheat salad with mushrooms, red onion, chopped parsley, and hazelnuts. Meals rich in plant foods and lean proteins provide compounds, fibers, and nutrients that fight inflammation.

[LIFESTYLE CHOICES]

There are many other factors that contribute to inflammation besides diet. For example, the process of aging stimulates the release of inflammatory compounds and accumulation of free radicals. The incidence of many inflammation-related conditions, such as Alzheimer's disease, heart disease, type 2 diabetes, and cancer, increases with age. Getting older is a natural part of life, but eating a nutritious diet can promote healthy aging.

In addition to aging, these non-dietary factors promote chronic inflammation:

- Lack of exercise
- Smoking
- Poor sleep
- Stress

It's important to address these factors when making dietary changes to fight inflammation. Following an anti-inflammatory style of eating can make a huge difference in managing health conditions. But the inflammatory effects of a sedentary lifestyle, cigarette smoking, high stress levels, or chronically poor sleep can dampen the progress you make with diet. Your efforts will be more beneficial if you make healthy lifestyle choices in addition to improving your food choices.

A NOTE ON HYDRATION

Dehydration is linked to chronic inflammation. Individuals with inflammatory diseases that affect the joints, such as rheumatoid arthritis, may have worse pain when they're dehydrated. This is because water helps lubricate the joints. Staying hydrated can help relieve joint pain and may also reduce overall inflammation. Besides drinking plenty of water, eat more foods with a high water content, such as cucumbers, watermelon, strawberries, oranges, lettuce, and cantaloupe.

Incorporate hydrating foods such as fruits and salad vegetables into your daily diet and aim to drink at least eight cups of water per day (opposite).

[INFLAMMATORY FOODS]

Certain foods can trigger inflammation in the body, possibly by stimulating the release of inflammatory compounds and compromising gut health. Limiting these types of foods may help calm chronic inflammation.

Possible inflammatory foods include:

- Foods with trans fats: fried foods, packaged baked goods, hydrogenated oils, refrigerated doughs, some frozen foods (such as mozzarella sticks), shortenings and margarines, pie crusts, microwave popcorn
- Fatty cuts of meat
- Cured and breakfast meats
- Refined sugars, such as those found in candy, sodas, and baked goods
- Pastries, doughnuts, cakes, cookies, and other products made with white flour or refined carbohydrates
- Alcohol

A NOTE ON SUGAR

Refined sugar can take many forms in food, and some manufacturers may "hide" it under different names. It may be listed as beet sugar, brown sugar, brown rice syrup, cane sugar, corn syrup solids, crystalline fructose, date sugar, evaporated cane juice, high-fructose corn syrup, invert sugar, maltodextrin, molasses, or turbinado sugar.

Since the ingredients of a product are listed by weight, using more than one type of sugar allows manufacturers to put them further down the list, even if they make up the majority of the product combined. Limit or avoid foods with "candied," "sugared," or "sweetened" in the name, and be wary of products marketed as "healthy desserts." Even though their clever marketing suggests otherwise, their food labels may reveal large amounts of added sugars, which can contribute to inflammation.

Although honey, agave nectar, and maple syrup count as sugar, they may not affect blood sugar as much as other types of sugar and offer some benefits, such as minerals and antioxidant compounds. See page 135 for more details about the use of honey in anti-inflammatory eating.

Above: Honey, agave nectar, and maple syrup are considered natural sweeteners, but they still count as sugar.

THE OMEGA-6 VS. OMEGA-3 DEBATE

Some experts speculate that overconsumption of omega-6 fatty acids, mainly due to the widespread use of highly refined vegetable and seed oils in the food supply, contributes to inflammation. Not getting enough omega-3 fatty acids may worsen the pro-inflammatory effect of consuming too much omega-6. However, most studies have found that omega-6 fatty acids do not actually worsen inflammation. Still, replacing highly refined vegetable and seed oils with extra-virgin olive oil is a beneficial swap for other reasons. Olive oil is loaded with antioxidants and has been shown to fight inflammation (see page 119). In addition, it's important to get omega-3s from fatty fish, plants, or supplements.

Above: Omega-3 is present in all forms of salmon. However, smoking, curing, and canning tend to yield more omega-3s per serving than fresh.

[ANTI-INFLAMMATORY FOODS]

While some foods trigger inflammation, others help fight it. Foods that provide antioxidants, beneficial compounds, omega-3 fatty acids, and/or fiber have anti-inflammatory potential. Increasing consumption of these foods appears to have a more significant effect on reducing chronic inflammation than cutting back on inflammatory foods.

Here is a general list of foods that contain inflammation-fighting nutrients and compounds:

- Vegetables
- Fruits
- Legumes
- Fatty fish
- Grains
- Nuts
- Seeds
- Olive oil
- Herbs and spices
- Fermented foods
- Dark chocolate
- Green tea

To reap the most benefits, aim to eat a varied diet that incorporates choices from all categories on this list, with an emphasis on fruits and vegetables (see page 25). This will help you supply your body with a variety of anti-inflammatory compounds. However, don't feel like you need to consume every item in order to fight chronic inflammation. If you don't enjoy green tea or kimchi, don't sweat it. Pick and choose from the foods you do enjoy. On the following pages, you will find a quick-reference chart to common foods grouped according to whether they rate as anti-inflammatory, neutral, or pro-inflammatory. This will help you to make informed decisions when planning your meals.

A NOTE ON CAFFEINE

Caffeine is often accused of being inflammatory, but that's not usually the case. Too much caffeine may lead to anxiety, insomnia, or gastrointestinal disturbances, especially if you are sensitive to it. In those instances, it's best to limit consumption. However, others do not experience negative side effects with caffeine. Plus, coffee consumption has actually been linked to health benefits and a reduced risk of disease, likely due to its high antioxidant content.

How you consume caffeine makes all the difference. Drinking coffee black or with a dash of cream or milk is not a concern, but using it as a vehicle for lots of added sugar may contribute to inflammation. Avoid sugary coffee drinks, such as flavored lattes and frappucinos, and caffeinated energy drinks with added sugars and artificial flavorings.

A bowl of oats soaked overnight in milk and served with fresh fruit makes for a good anti-inflammatory breakfast.

[AT-A-GLANCE FOOD CHART]

Check through these lists to see which foods are anti-inflammatory, which are neutral, and which are pro-inflammatory.

	VEGETABLES	FRUIT	GRAINS AND FLOURS
ANTI-INFLAMMATORY FOODS	All fresh vegetables—eaten raw or simply cooked	All fresh fruits—eaten raw or cooked without added sugar	Oats, whole grains (such as brown and wild rice), quinoa, 100% whole grain flours such as those made from whole wheat, oats, or spelt
NEUTRAL FOODS	Starchy vegetables such as potatoes and corn offer beneficial nutrients but can spike blood sugar in large amounts	Dried fruits, though rich in nutrients and fiber, are easy to overeat and can spike blood sugar	White rice has less fiber than whole grains and should be used less frequently
PRO-INFLAMMATORY FOODS	All fried vegetables; stuffed vegetables with too much cheese or bacon; vegetable juices with added sugars; carrot cakes and zucchini breads that are high in sugar and fat	Canned fruits in syrup, sweetened dried fruits, candied fruits, fruit juices and smoothies with added sugars	Large amounts of white flour and products made from refined grains, such as noodles, white bread, bagels, pies, pastries, and baked goods

PROTEINS	FATS	SWEETS	DRINKS
Fatty fish, legumes, whole soy products, unsweetened Greek yogurt	Raw or oven-roasted nuts and seeds, extra-virgin olive oil, avocado and avocado oil, fatty fish	Dark chocolate, raw honey and pure maple syrup used in moderation and in place of refined sweeteners, fruits	Water, green or black tea, smoothies made with whole fruits and vegetables
Lean cuts of meat, eggs	Cheeses, coconut oil or seed oils used in moderation	Healthier baked goods or treats, made with less sugar and whole grain flours	100% vegetable or fruit juice, coffee, herbal teas
Breakfast meats, fast food burgers and sandwiches, cured meats, fatty cuts of meat, highly processed faux meats	Candied nuts, trans-fats, highly processed cheese spreads and cheese "wiz"	Sweets made with refined sugars and carbohydrates, ice cream, candy, sodas	Excess alcohol, sodas, sugar-laden juices or smoothies, energy drinks

[A BLUEPRINT FOR ANTI-INFLAMMATORY EATING]

As you browse through this book, you'll notice that there are no strict rules or guidelines associated with an anti-inflammatory diet. Eating to fight inflammation is more about the addition of foods to your diet rather than restriction. Dietary patterns that have been associated with anti-inflammatory benefits, including the Mediterranean diet and diets that fall under the Dietary Approaches to Stop Hypertension (DASH) umbrella, share many commonalities. They are predominantly plant-based and mostly composed of vegetables and fruits, emphasize healthy fats such as fish, nuts, and olive oil, and encourage limited or moderate consumption of alcohol, high-fat animal foods, and added sugar. These guiding principles are the basis of nearly every eating pattern associated with good health, and anti-inflammatory eating is no exception.

Explore the 50 foods in this book with those principles in mind. Get excited about how you can experiment with anti-inflammatory foods, and challenge yourself to try new recipes with them. By focusing on the new additions to your diet, you may find that you naturally begin to eat less of the foods that contribute to inflammation without even focusing on restriction. Baked sweet potatoes may replace French fries, and oatmeal with fresh berries may replace a bowl of sugary cereal. With no strict rules, anti-inflammatory eating allows room for your favorite treat or a glass of wine, but perhaps these indulgences will be more on occasion than regular features.

A serving of fresh strawberries could contribute to your half-plate of fruits and vegetables or could make up an easy meal booster with a spoonful of yogurt.

THE ANTI-INFLAMMATORY PLATE

As you get started with a new style of eating, it can be helpful to have some type of blueprint to follow.

With each meal you prepare, consider your different food types in the proportions outlined below. This is a very useful guide to putting together meals with anti-inflammatory foods.

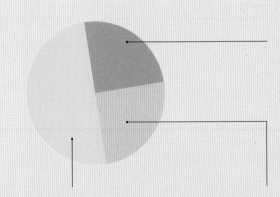

25% Lean Protein or Fatty Fish

- Choose mostly fatty fish or legumes and other plant-based proteins
- Eat fatty fish twice a week
- Incorporate eggs and lean cuts of meat in moderation

25% Complex Carbohydrates

- Serve whole grains, 100% whole grain or legume-based pasta, or sweet potatoes
- Fruit or legumes can also make up this part of the plate

50% Fruits and Vegetables

- Eat leafy greens at one or more meals on most days
- Incorporate five or more servings of cruciferous vegetables per week
- Add berries to your plate two or more times per week
- Use a variety of other fruits and vegetables to make up the rest of your intake

MEALTIME EXTRAS

Healthy fats
- Add 1 oz of nuts or seeds
- Add 1 to 2 tbsp nut butter or olive oil
- Add avocado
- Eat fatty fish

What to drink?
- Water
- Green or black tea
- Limit alcohol to two drinks per day for men; one drink per day for women (or less!)

Easy meal boosters
- A spoonful of sauerkraut or kimchi
- Cook with miso
- Use yogurt-based condiments
- Add herbs and spices
- Finish your meal with dark chocolate

[SPECIAL DIETS]

The principles of anti-inflammatory eating can be incorporated into special diets. If you follow a specific diet, or have been advised to eat in a certain way for medical reasons, there may be some anti-inflammatory foods that are not suitable for your needs. Here are some of the most common special diets and points to consider. Each food type discussed in the following chapter includes information pertaining to special diets.

KETOGENIC DIET

A ketogenic, or keto, diet drastically reduces carbohydrates while increasing fat consumption. Fruits, legumes, whole grains, and starchy vegetables such as sweet potatoes are generally restricted on a keto diet. However, many other anti-inflammatory foods are permitted, including nuts, seeds, extra-virgin olive oil, fatty fish, and non-starchy vegetables.

LOW-GI OR DIABETES-FRIENDLY DIETS

If you have diabetes or issues with blood sugar regulation, you may be advised to eat foods with low glycemic indexes (GI) to avoid spikes in blood sugar. It's also advisable to avoid large portions of high-carbohydrate foods and pair carbohydrates with sources of protein, healthy fat, and fiber. Most of the foods in this book can be enjoyed by those who are conscious about carbohydrates and GI as part of a balanced diet. The key is to be mindful of your portions of foods such as sweet potatoes and other starchy vegetables, fruits, grains, beans, and honey. Aim to eat whole fruits over drinking fruit juice.

Protein-rich foods such as chicken and eggs can give bulk to those eating salad-based meals as part of a gluten-free diet.

GLUTEN-FREE DIET

Individuals with celiac disease or gluten sensitivity need to follow a gluten-free diet. This diet eliminates all gluten-containing grains, such as wheat and barley, and products made with gluten. Almost all of the foods in this book are gluten-free, but there are some exceptions to consider. Some whole grains are not gluten-free. Oats and quinoa do not naturally contain gluten but may be contaminated with gluten-containing grains during processing. Other foods, such as miso paste, may be made with ingredients that contain gluten. Look for products labeled as certified gluten-free if you need to avoid gluten.

VEGAN OR VEGETARIAN DIETS

Vegetarian diets exclude meat and fish and may restrict eggs or dairy products, while vegan diets eliminate all animal products. The directory of foods in this book is predominantly plant-based. Most of them can be included on vegan and vegetarian diets, with the exception of fatty fish and yogurt. Legumes, soy products such as tofu and edamame, nuts, and seeds are all good sources of protein for those following fully plant-based eating patterns.

Rice noodles (opposite) and pancakes paired with vegetables make ideal meals for vegetarians and those on low-GI diets.

TIPS FOR EATING OUT

Following an anti-inflammatory style of eating doesn't mean you have to give up going out to eat, but it can make the process more challenging. These suggestions will help you navigate restaurant menus to find a dish that fits into your eating pattern. To be fully prepared, browse the menu online before you get to the restaurant.

- **Spot the vegetables:** Look for meals that are centered around vegetables. Salads or vegetable soups are a great place to start, but you may find some plant-based entrées, too. If you opt for salad, choose one with a base of leafy greens and nutritious toppings such as avocado, fruit, nuts, or seeds. Ask the server what's in a dressing, and request olive oil and vinegar on the side if it's made with high-fat or sugary ingredients. If the restaurant offers a veggie burger, see if the full ingredients are listed. Some places may offer house-made options that use beans, whole grains, and other nutritious ingredients. Bowl meals made with whole grains and vegetables are becoming popular menu options and can be a good choice, too.

A vegetable-based soup can make a good entrée to an anti-inflammatory restaurant meal.

- **Check out the fish:** Many restaurants offer a seafood entrée served with vegetables. This is a great option as long as the fish isn't deep-fried or smothered in a heavy sauce. If salmon is a choice, order a plate of those omega-3 fats (see opposite)!

- **Read the fine print:** Some meals may be deep-fried or served with foods that contribute to inflammation, such as heavy sauces, white bread and rolls, pasta, white rice, or French fries. Be sure to read the descriptions of menu items and ask the server if you are unsure what's included. Avoid options with fried, smothered, rich, or breaded in the description. Ask if you can upgrade sides like French fries, chips, or bread to a salad, soup, fruit, or vegetables. If a meal is served with rice, ask for brown instead of white.

When choosing salads, lean proteins such as chicken breast, beans, or egg can round out a meal so you are not left feeling hungry or unsatisfied.

- **Be careful with breakfast:** Breakfast meals are often served with white toast and sugary jams or processed meats such as bacon and sausage, all of which can contribute to inflammation. When ordering options that come with these sides, ask to hold the meat. See if you can substitute fruit for the toast or choose 100% whole grain bread.

[FREQUENTLY ASKED QUESTIONS]

Anyone planning to adopt an anti-inflammatory diet will have questions, and here are some of the most common. If in doubt, consult with a registered dietician or health care provider.

DO I NEED TO AVOID GLUTEN?

You may have heard that gluten is pro-inflammatory and should be avoided on an anti-inflammatory diet. However, if you don't have celiac disease or gluten sensitivity, this is likely not true. An anti-inflammatory diet that's predominantly based on the foods in this book would be almost entirely gluten-free. For example, vegetables and fruits naturally do not contain gluten and are the cornerstone of anti-inflammatory eating. But the lack of gluten in anti-inflammatory foods doesn't mean that gluten itself is pro-inflammatory.

What's more, there are many gluten-free products that are heavily processed, high in sugar, and offer minimal nutritional value. Choosing a gluten-free cookie over a regular cookie is not an inherently healthier choice. If you believe that gluten-containing foods make you feel ill or cause digestive issues, a health care provider and registered dietitian can evaluate your situation and advise on whether you need to follow a gluten-free diet. And remember, eating a diet centered on the foods in this book means that you won't consume much (if any) gluten anyways.

DO I NEED TO AVOID DAIRY?

The research on dairy and inflammation has been mixed and inconclusive. Yogurt, with its abundance of beneficial probiotics, is considered an anti-inflammatory food. However, the effect of other types of dairy foods is less clear. Since foods that are high in saturated fat have been linked to inflammation, full-fat dairy products are probably not the best addition to anti-inflammatory meals. But eating foods with dairy on occasion likely won't jeopardize your efforts. If you have lactose intolerance or do not feel your best after eating dairy, avoid or limit dairy products.

DO I NEED TO COMPLETELY ELIMINATE ALCOHOL?

Overconsumption of alcohol can disrupt the lining of the gut, which over time may cause irritants to "leak" from the gut into the body and promote inflammation. Drinking too much alcohol may also contribute to weight gain and an increased risk of some inflammation-related diseases. For these reasons, it's best to limit alcohol consumption when following an anti-inflammatory diet. Drink alcohol in moderation, which most experts define as one drink per day for women and two drinks per day for men. Less frequent consumption may be even more beneficial, especially in the first few weeks or months of trying anti-inflammatory eating. For reference, a standard drink is defined as 12 oz of beer, 5 oz of wine, and 1.5 oz of hard liquor.

While dairy products should not be problematic to most people following an anti-inflammatory diet, it is best to opt for low-fat options where possible.

IS ORGANIC PRODUCE BETTER THAN CONVENTIONAL?

Organic farming uses fewer pesticides and implements techniques that are typically more beneficial for the environment than conventional farming. There is an ongoing debate about whether or not pesticides are harmful to human health. While it's possible that some pesticides present health risks in very high doses, the residue levels on conventional produce are considered negligible by many experts and well below the recommended safe limits.

Increasing fruit and vegetable intake is connected to countless benefits and can help fight inflammation. All types of produce—organic, conventional, fresh, frozen, and even canned (choose no-added-salt vegetables and fruit canned in its juice instead of syrup)—are great options, depending on your needs and preferences. If you prefer organic produce and want to support organic farming techniques, look for the USDA certified organic logo on fruits and vegetables before purchasing. Wash or rinse all produce before eating to remove dirt, bacteria, and pesticide residue.

If you choose to eat bread as part of your anti-inflammatory diet, be sure to eat varieties made with whole grains.

ANTI-INFLAMMATORY
FOODS

Now that you understand the basics of anti-inflammatory eating, it's time to discuss the best foods to incorporate into your diet. The following pages explore 50 of the top foods for fighting inflammation and supporting your body's anti-inflammatory responses.

The section begins with vegetables and fruits that are rich in micronutrients, antioxidants, fiber, and a variety of compounds that suppress inflammation, including flavonoids and carotenoids. Next, you will learn about whole grains, legumes, fish, nuts, seeds, and oils that have anti-inflammatory properties. The concluding pages cover herbs and spices, beverages, chocolate, and fermented foods— meal "boosters" that can raise the inflammation-fighting potential of your plate.

[LEAFY GREENS]

- A BURST OF VITAMIN C -

Leafy green vegetables include lettuce, spinach, collard greens, Swiss chard, cabbage, watercress, mustard greens, turnip greens, arugula, and kale, among others, many of which are also cruciferous vegetables (see pages 36–39). Most are rich in antioxidants, such as provitamin A carotenoids and vitamin C, and plant compounds that help fight inflammation, such as lutein.

Choosing Leafy Greens

The freshest greens have crisp, unbroken leaves with a solid dark green color and no signs of wilting. Swiss chard, collard greens, and kale are known to have a strong, bitter taste. Arugula and mustard greens offer a spicy kick, and spinach and lettuces are milder.

In the Kitchen

Some nutrients that contribute to the anti-inflammatory properties of leafy greens are heat-sensitive and water-soluble. To preserve vitamin C in greens, eat them raw or lightly steamed. Serve greens with a source of fat, such as avocado or olive oil, to boost absorption of fat-soluble vitamin A and lutein.

HOW TO EAT MORE

- *Blend into smoothies with frozen fruits and/or yogurt*
- *Replace tortillas with collard greens as an alternative to wraps and burritos*
- *Stir shredded greens into soups, omelets, or stir-fries*

DID YOU KNOW?

Stems from kale, collard greens, chard, or mustard greens are edible. Add them to sautéed vegetable dishes, blend them in juices and smoothies, or pickle them.

NUTRITION PER
2 CUPS CHOPPED, RAW KALE

Calories	18
Fat	0.7 g
Protein	1.4 g
Carbohydrates	2.2 g
Fiber	2 g
Natural sugars	0.2 g
Sodium	26 mg
Potassium	174 mg

LEAFY GREENS AND YOUR DIET

Leafy greens make an excellent addition to vegan, vegetarian, keto, gluten-free, and diabetes-friendly eating plans.

Individuals with high blood pressure can benefit from eating more greens, as they are naturally low in sodium and are often a good source of potassium. Getting enough potassium from foods, while keeping sodium in check, is often recommended for maintaining healthy blood pressure. The anti-inflammatory compounds in leafy greens may soothe inflammation linked to heart disease.

Greens are rich in vitamin K (the blood-clotting vitamin), so individuals on blood-thinning medications should check with a doctor before increasing intake of leafy greens. If you have a history of kidney stones, exercise caution with spinach and beet greens. Each contains high levels of oxalates that may contribute to stone development. For those with inflammatory bowel disease (IBD), raw greens may worsen symptoms.

[CRUCIFEROUS VEGETABLES]

- ANTIOXIDANT BRASSICAS -

Cruciferous is a term used for vegetables that belong to the Brassicaceae, or mustard, family of plants. These include broccoli, cauliflower, Brussels sprouts, broccoli rabe (rapini), radishes, cabbage, kohlrabi, rutabaga, and turnips. Many leafy greens, such as arugula, bok choy, chard, collard greens, kale, mustard greens, and watercress, also belong to this family. Cruciferous vegetables tend to have a strong aroma and some have a sharp, bitter, or spicy taste.

These vegetables provide sulfur-containing compounds known as glucosinolates, which break down to isothiocyanates and may exhibit anti-inflammatory and anti-cancer effects. Some cruciferous vegetables, such as broccoli, Brussels sprouts, and cabbage, contain kaempferol, a potent anti-inflammatory compound. In addition, cruciferous vegetables are often rich in provitamin A carotenoids and vitamin C, which act as antioxidants.

Choosing Cruciferous Vegetables

When choosing heads of broccoli or cauliflower, look for firm stalks and tight florets that do not have black or brown spots. Brussels sprouts should be free of yellow leaves and discoloration, while radishes should feel firm to the touch and have bright-green leaves. The freshest heads of cabbage will have tightly packed leaves that are not wilted. For kohlrabi, rutabaga, and turnips, make sure their skins are unblemished. These vegetables may have some cracks around the top, but they shouldn't appear on other parts of the skin.

NUTRITION PER
2 CUPS RAW CAULIFLOWER FLORETS

Calories	54
Fat	0.6 g
Protein	4.2 g
Carbohydrates	10 g
Fiber	4.2 g
Natural sugars	4 g
Sodium	64 mg
Potassium	640 mg

HOW TO EAT MORE

- *Combine shredded Brussels sprouts with dried fruit, chopped nuts, and a lemon and olive oil dressing*

- *Add broccoli and cauliflower florets to stir-fries, or turn them into "rice" using a food processor*

- *Turn kohlrabi, rutabaga, or turnips into "noodles" using a spiralizer, and serve in place of pasta*

- *Thinly slice radishes and add to salads*

- *Use shredded cabbage as a base for healthy coleslaw, tossed in Greek yogurt or olive-oil-based dressing*

In the Kitchen

Aim to eat a mix of raw and gently cooked vegetables from this group. Research continues to explore the effects of cooking methods on the anti-inflammatory compounds in cruciferous vegetables, and the results are still inconclusive.

Eating cruciferous vegetables raw preserves some of their anti-inflammatory nutrients, such as vitamin C, glucosinolates, and other plant compounds. However, some cooking methods may actually increase the content of isothiocyanates, which come from glucosinolates and are responsible for many of the benefits associated with them.

Steaming, stir-frying, microwaving, and other light cooking methods, have been shown to increase isothiocyanate yields in cruciferous vegetables. Boiling and stewing, on the other hand, reduce these yields.

Cruciferous Vegetables and Your Diet

Cruciferous vegetables can be enjoyed on vegan, vegetarian, gluten-free, and low-carb diets. They are generally well tolerated and full of nutrients and fiber, while remaining low in carbohydrates and calories. However, eating a lot of cruciferous vegetables can lead to stomach discomfort, bloating, or gas for some people, especially for those with digestive issues.

Individuals with hypothyroidism or Hashimoto's disease may want to limit their consumption and cook cruciferous vegetables instead of consuming them raw. Cruciferous vegetables contain goitrogens, which may interfere with the functioning of the thyroid gland at high doses. Consuming them in moderation is unlikely to be a concern, but check with your health care provider if you have thyroid issues.

Finally, if you are on blood-thinning medication, avoid drastically increasing consumption of cruciferous vegetables. Many of them are high in vitamin K, a nutrient that helps with blood clotting. Individuals on blood-thinning medications are advised to keep vitamin K intake consistent and should consult with a health care provider about dietary changes that affect vitamin K levels.

VARIETIES TO TRY

- *Cauliflower: Mild-tasting, with white, yellow, purple, and green varieties*
- *Broccoli: Quick-cooking and versatile, with a grassy flavor*
- *Arugula: Adds a pop of color and a spicy, peppery kick to dishes*
- *Watercress: Has an intense, peppery taste that lends itself to being used like an herb*
- *Kohlrabi: Tastes like broccoli stalks and can be enjoyed raw, roasted, or sautéed*
- *Radishes: Red radishes are zesty and spicy; white, daikon radishes are milder*
- *Rutabaga: Mashed rutabaga makes a good lower-carb alternative to potato*
- *Mustard greens: Have a sharp taste resembling the condiment with which they share a name*
- *Turnips: Slice into "fries" and roast to mellow their bitter flavor*
- *Kale: A robust leafy green with a strong, earthy taste*

DID YOU KNOW?

Maca root is a cruciferous vegetable grown in Peru. Available in powder form, it can be stirred into smoothies, energy bites, and oatmeal.

Opposite, clockwise from top: Cauliflower brings a brassica boost to a vegan lunch; Brussels sprouts are simply roasted with herbs; a bunch of fresh radishes.

[SWEET POTATOES]

Sweet potatoes contain a plethora of nutrients and compounds that fight inflammation. They're loaded with vitamin C and rich in beta-carotene, the pigment that gives them their beautiful orange color and gets converted to vitamin A in the body. These nutrients act as antioxidants, helping to balance out damaging free radicals that can contribute to disease development.

Choosing Sweet Potatoes

Sweet potatoes should feel firm to the touch and be without bruises or wrinkles. The smaller the potato, the sweeter it will taste. Don't be afraid to stock up on sweet potatoes, especially if they're on offer, since they can last for up to two weeks in a cool, dry place.

In the Kitchen

Sweet potatoes can lose nutrients when exposed to heat for long periods of time. To preserve as much beta-carotene and vitamin C as possible, keep the skin on and limit the cooking time. Steaming or boiling sweet potatoes is better than roasting, at least when it comes to nutrients that are not water-soluble, since the cooking time doesn't have to be as long.

HOW TO EAT MORE

- *Mash and serve with olive oil, sage, cinnamon, and a touch of maple syrup*
- *Swap breads, bagels, or pastries for sautéed sweet potatoes at breakfast*
- *Boil or steam cubes to blend into smoothies*

DID YOU KNOW?

Not all sweet potatoes are orange! Purple sweet potatoes are particularly concentrated sources of anthocyanins, the pigments that give them their color and help mitigate inflammatory processes.

NUTRITION PER
1 CUP CUBED, RAW SWEET POTATO

Calories	114
Fat	0.1 g
Protein	2.1 g
Carbohydrates	27 g
Fiber	4 g
Natural sugars	6 g
Sodium	3 mg
Potassium	448 mg

SWEET POTATOES AND YOUR DIET

Sweet potatoes can be added to vegan, vegetarian, and gluten-free eating patterns. They are not as suitable for keto or very low-carb diets, since they're higher in carbohydrates than non-starchy vegetables.

Individuals with diabetes can enjoy sweet potatoes as a healthy source of complex carbohydrates, but should consider how they're cooked. Some cooking methods may cause sweet potatoes to raise blood sugar levels more than others. To support good blood sugar control, it's best to boil sweet potatoes instead of roasting, baking, or frying them.

Sweet potatoes are served for holiday meals, with marshmallows, brown sugar, and/or lots of butter, and make a delicious treat to eat on occasion. But keep in mind that these preparations of sweet potatoes do not fit well into an anti-inflammatory diet, especially if you have heart disease or diabetes.

[CARROTS]

- LOADED WITH LUTEIN -

Carrots are chock full of anti-inflammatory substances, including beta-carotene, lutein, and polyacetylenes. Purple carrots also contain anthocyanins, while red carrots have lycopene. These compounds may act in a variety of ways to mitigate inflammatory processes in the body. Carrot juice, in particular, has been the subject of preliminary rodent studies for its potential in protecting against inflammatory liver conditions.

Choosing Carrots

Look for brightly colored carrots with unbruised, firm skin and vibrant green leaves (if attached). Carrots are available in several different colors that taste virtually the same. However, non-orange carrots tend to lose their color during cooking.

In the Kitchen

Cooking carrots appears to improve absorption of beta-carotene. In fact, even if some beta-carotene is lost due to heat exposure, the increase in accessibility makes up for it. To further boost absorption of beta-carotene, serve carrots with a source of healthy fat.

HOW TO EAT MORE

- *Eat baby carrots with hummus or a yogurt dip*
- *Slice carrots into "fries," roast, and serve with a lemon tahini sauce*
- *Add shredded carrots to muffins, breads, and other baked goods*

DID YOU KNOW?

Large carrots can be made into "noodles" and used as a gluten-free substitute for pasta.

NUTRITION PER
1 MEDIUM RAW CARROT

Calories	25
Fat	0.1 g
Protein	0.6 g
Carbohydrates	6 g
Fiber	1.7 g
Natural sugars	2.9 g
Sodium	42 mg
Potassium	195 mg

CARROTS AND YOUR DIET

Carrots are one of the most popular vegetables and fit into almost every eating pattern. Due to their pleasing taste, carrots are a good option for those who are just starting out with anti-inflammatory eating and gradually increasing vegetable intake.

The inflammation-fighting properties of carrots may be beneficial for those with heart disease, high blood pressure, arthritis, nonalcoholic fatty liver disease (NAFLD), and other conditions related to chronic inflammation.

Carrots are sometimes accused of being "too high" in sugar, but their sugars are all natural and their total carbohydrate content remains low. Plus, they're a good source of dietary fiber. If you are watching your carbohydrate intake, just keep an eye on how many carrots you consume since their carb content can add up with large quantities.

[MUSHROOMS]

– POLYSACCHARIDE POWERHOUSES –

Mushrooms have long been used in traditional and folk medicines. The main anti-inflammatory compounds in fungi are polysaccharides, terpenoids, peptides, and phenols.

Choosing Mushrooms

The anti-inflammatory potential of mushrooms differs from one variety to the next, with reishi among those offering the greatest benefits. Shiitake, portabello, chanterelle, porcini, and oyster are some of the tastiest. Choose firm mushrooms, and avoid slimy or dry ones. Mushroom powders and extracts tend to be more potent than whole mushrooms used in cooking. High in anti-inflammatory activity, they may be derived from reishi, lion's mane, maitake, shiitake, or turkey tail mushrooms.

In the Kitchen

To preserve the anti-inflammatory capacity of mushrooms, eat them raw or use gentle cooking methods, such as steaming or stir-frying for a short time. Avoid adding a lot of liquid during cooking, which can cause mushrooms to become soggy.

HOW TO EAT MORE

- Use portabello mushrooms as plant-based "burgers" or stuff them with brown rice and vegetables
- Stir mushroom powders into smoothies and soups
- Combine chickpea noodles, sautéed mushrooms, garlic, kale, and olive oil for a quick dinner

DID YOU KNOW?

Fresh mushrooms keep best when stored in a brown paper bag in the refrigerator. Dried and dehydrated mushrooms have a much longer shelf life and make great additions to last-minute meals.

NUTRITION PER
1 CUP SLICED, RAW MUSHROOMS

Calories	16
Fat	0.2 g
Protein	2.2 g
Carbohydrates	2.3 g
Fiber	0.7 g
Natural sugars	1.4 g
Sodium	4 mg
Potassium	223 mg

MUSHROOMS AND YOUR DIET

Adding mushrooms to your meals is an easy way to reap anti-inflammatory benefits, even if you follow a low-carb, gluten-free, vegan, or vegetarian diet.

There are virtually no negative effects from eating commonly available culinary mushrooms in moderation, but there may be some concerns with medicinal mushrooms and powders. Some people may experience mild side effects, such as an upset stomach, when taking these mushrooms. There is also a concern that medicinal mushrooms may lead to liver toxicity when taken for extended periods of time. Speak to a doctor before trying mushroom supplements, especially if you are pregnant or breastfeeding or are taking immunosuppressants, chemotherapy medications, blood thinners, or blood pressure medications.

There is very limited evidence to support claims that reishi mushrooms and other mushroom powders and extracts boost immunity and thereby help fight cancer.

[BEETS]

The gorgeous color of beets is an indication of their anti-inflammatory potential. They get their deep red hue from pigments known as betalains, which act as antioxidants. They also contain betaine, a compound that may reduce inflammatory markers associated with heart disease, kidney disease, arthritis, and diabetes.

Choosing Beets

Beets should be firm and void of dark bruises. Red beets are the most popular, but golden, Chioggia (with pink and white striped flesh), and even white beets are also available. If intact, greens should show no signs of wilting or damage. To save time, look for packaged, pre-cooked beets in the produce section.

In the Kitchen

To maintain the betalain content of beets, eat them raw or steam them for up to 15 minutes. Cooking, especially boiling, also leads to loss of betaine. When preparing beets, they can stain your hands. The red tint will fade and come off after a few good scrubs.

HOW TO EAT MORE

- *Grate raw beets and use in slaws or turn into "noodles" using a spiralizer*
- *Steam beets and serve them with goat cheese, olive oil, and lemon juice*
- *Thinly slice Chioggia beets and combine with carrots and a dressing of mint, parsley, orange juice, honey, and olive oil for a pretty salad*

DID YOU KNOW?

Even though they don't have the quintessential red color of their more popular counterpart, golden beets also contain betalains.

NUTRITION PER
1 MEDIUM RAW BEET

Calories	35
Fat	0.1 g
Protein	1.3 g
Carbohydrates	8 g
Fiber	2.3 g
Natural sugars	6 g
Sodium	64 mg
Potassium	267 mg

BEETS AND YOUR DIET

Beets are naturally gluten-free, vegan, and vegetarian. Like carrots, they are higher in natural sugars than most other vegetables. However, they offer slow-burning carbohydrates and fiber and are not a concern for those on low-carb diets when consumed in moderation.

This colorful root vegetable is an all-star addition to your anti-inflammatory meals and even offers some extra benefits for those with high blood pressure. Beets contain nitrates, which get converted to nitric oxide in the body and help relax blood vessels. Individuals with diabetes are encouraged to eat beets, as they contain nutrients that may lower the risk of some diabetes complications.

However, beets may not be the best anti-inflammatory choice for everyone. Since they contain oxalates that contribute to the development of kidney stones, those with a history of stones should limit their beet consumption.

[ARTICHOKES]

One of the most antioxidant-rich foods, the artichoke is a source of potent anti-inflammatory compounds, such as cynarin and cynaropicrin. Artichokes are also an excellent source of dietary fiber. High-fiber foods feed healthy bacteria in the gut, leading to the release of substances that reduce inflammation in the body.

Choosing Artichokes

To check an artichoke's freshness, give it a squeeze and see if it squeaks—an indication that the leaves are succulent and not dried out. Canned artichoke hearts are an affordable, shelf-stable, and time-saving option, but they don't include the nutrient-rich leaves.

In the Kitchen

Most parts of a cooked artichoke are edible, including the leaves, stem, and heart. Use your teeth to scrape away the tender flesh at the base of the outer leaves and eat the soft inner leaves and the heart whole. Discard the fuzzy choke at the center. Steaming and boiling make an artichoke's antioxidant compounds more accessible than other cooking methods.

HOW TO EAT MORE

- *Dip tender artichoke leaves in a sauce of lemon juice combined with olive oil or Greek yogurt, Dijon mustard, and fresh herbs*
- *Sauté artichoke hearts with shrimp in lemon juice, olive oil, garlic, and parsley, and serve over brown rice*
- *Add artichoke hearts to salads*

DID YOU KNOW?

Rubbing fresh lemon juice onto cut surfaces during preparation prevents artichokes from going brown.

NUTRITION PER
1 MEDIUM ARTICHOKE

Calories	60
Fat	0.2 g
Protein	4.2 g
Carbohydrates	13 g
Fiber	7 g
Natural sugars	1.3 g
Sodium	20 mg
Potassium:	474 mg

ARTICHOKES AND YOUR DIET

With so much fiber and anti-inflammatory potential, artichokes are an excellent food to add to all sorts of eating patterns. They fit into gluten-free, vegan, vegetarian, low-carb, heart-healthy, and diabetes-friendly diets.

Research has explored the benefits of artichokes for many diseases associated with chronic inflammation, including liver and heart diseases. They may also help with lowering blood sugar levels in individuals with diabetes.

Due to their high fiber content, however, artichokes may cause gas, stomach discomfort, or diarrhea in some people and those with digestive issues. If you are trying artichokes for the first time, start with a small portion, monitor your symptoms, and gradually add more artichokes to your diet if well tolerated.

[FENNEL]

Fennel is a green and white bulbous vegetable with a licorice-like flavor. Both the bulb and seeds contain anti-inflammatory plant compounds, including the antioxidant quercetin and the compound anethole. Fennel is also thought to help with digestive issues and symptoms of IBD, though research on these benefits is still limited.

Choosing Fennel

Fennel bulbs should be firm and bruise-free, with rigid stalks. You may also come across fennel with its feathery green fronds attached. These can be used as a garnish or seasoning in a similar way to fresh herbs. Fennel seeds are available in the spice aisle or through online retailers.

In the Kitchen

Not much is known about the effects of cooking on the anti-inflammatory potential of fennel. Enjoying both raw and cooked fennel appears to offer benefits. When preparing fennel, slice the bulb into quarters, remove the core from each piece, then rinse the layers under cold water to remove any hidden dirt.

HOW TO EAT MORE

- *Simmer fennel in vegetable broth or coconut milk and use to braise seafood*
- *Roast fennel with cherry tomatoes and serve over lentil pasta*
- *Use fennel seeds to make tea*

DID YOU KNOW?

Sipping fennel tea or chewing on fennel seeds may help freshen up your breath. This likely has to do with its anti-bacterial properties.

NUTRITION PER
1 CUP SLICED, RAW FENNEL

Calories	27
Fat	0.2 g
Protein	1.1 g
Carbohydrates	6 g
Fiber	2.7 g
Natural sugars	3.4 g
Sodium	45 mg
Potassium	360 mg

FENNEL AND YOUR DIET

Fennel is naturally gluten-free, vegan, and vegetarian. Since fennel is low in carbs and a good source of dietary fiber, it can help those with diabetes maintain good blood sugar control. The antioxidants, fiber, and other heart-healthy nutrients also make it a fitting choice for individuals with heart disease.

Those with IBD or irritable bowel syndrome (IBS) may benefit from fennel as well. There are many anecdotes that endorse drinking fennel tea to relieve digestive discomfort, but research on fennel tea and supplements is scarce. Moreover, fennel tea may not be recommended for those following a low FODMAP (fermentable oligosaccharides, disaccharides, monosaccharides and polyols) diet plan.

[CELERY]

It's true that celery is mostly water, but this hydrating stalk still packs a lot of anti-inflammatory compounds. Celery contains a variety of flavonoids, including the antioxidant quercetin, which protect cells from damage associated with disease development. Apiuman, a polysaccharide found in celery, may inhibit the production of proteins that signal inflammation.

Choosing Celery

Celery stalks should be crisp and green. Limp, bruised, or dry celery is past its prime. To preserve freshness, whole celery stalks should be wrapped in foil and stored in the crisper drawer in the refrigerator. Stalks that have already been cut can be placed in cold water in an airtight container in the refrigerator.

In the Kitchen

Cooking celery, via baking, stir-frying, microwaving, or pressure-cooking, but not boiling, has been shown to increase its antioxidant potential.

HOW TO EAT MORE

- *Stuff stalks with almond or sunflower seed butter and top with raisins*
- *Roast celery with olive oil, salt, pepper, and herbs*
- *Make a healthier version of cream of celery soup using Greek yogurt*

DID YOU KNOW?

Juicing celery takes away the beneficial fiber that helps feed healthy gut bacteria, which assist in regulating anti-inflammatory activity in the body.

NUTRITION PER
1 MEDIUM RAW STALK

Calories	5.6
Fat	0.1 g
Protein	0.3 g
Carbohydrates	1.2 g
Fiber	0.6 g
Natural sugars	0.5 g
Sodium	32 mg
Potassium	104 mg

CELERY AND YOUR DIET

Celery fits into nearly any special diet, including vegan, vegetarian, gluten-free, and low-carb eating patterns. It's very filling and makes a healthy, anti-inflammatory addition to meals.

Those with type 2 diabetes may benefit from celery's inflammation-fighting potential. Quercetin found in celery may help lower blood sugar levels by increasing insulin secretion and promoting glucose uptake by the liver.

However, it's important to eat celery in moderation. Going overboard with celery, especially in the form of highly concentrated celery juice, may have unwanted side effects if you are on certain medications. Since celery provides a decent amount of vitamin K, consuming a large amount of it (as in juice) may interfere with blood thinners (see page 35).

[CHICORIES]

Chicories are a group of lettuce-like vegetables with mild bitter tastes that mellow through cooking. The chicory family includes Belgian endive, frisée (curly endive), radicchio, and escarole. These vegetables are full of antioxidants and inflammation-fighting compounds, including the anthocyanins that give radicchio its purple color and the flavonoid kaempferol in endive.

Choosing Chicories

Avoid chicories that are wilted or bruised. When choosing Belgian endive, look for tightly packed leaves. To prolong its freshness, shield endive from light by wrapping it in paper towels before placing in a bag or container in the refrigerator.

In the Kitchen

Eating chicories raw or cooking them quickly is the best way to preserve anti-inflammatory nutrients. If the bitter taste of raw chicories isn't for you, try steaming or quick sautéing. You may also enjoy milder chicories, such as frisée and escarole, over radicchio and endive.

HOW TO EAT MORE

- *Make a frisée salad with Dijon vinaigrette*
- *Stuff Belgian endive leaves with a healthy dip for a snack*
- *Cook chopped escarole with white beans, lemon juice, and red pepper flakes*

DID YOU KNOW?

The root of chicory plants also has anti-inflammatory properties. Chicory root contains inulin, a prebiotic fiber that feeds healthy bacteria in your gut.

NUTRITION PER
1 CUP SHREDDED, RAW RADICCHIO

Calories	9
Fat	0.1 g
Protein	0.6 g
Carbohydrates	1.8 g
Fiber	0.4 g
Natural sugars	0.2 g
Sodium	8.8 mg
Potassium	121 mg

CHICORIES AND YOUR DIET

Eating more chicory vegetables is a fun way to mix up your leafy green intake. They offer unique tastes that set them apart from commonly consumed salad greens. Plus, chicories can be enjoyed on all types of special diets.

Preliminary studies in animals suggest that eating chicories helps reduce inflammation associated with heart disease and plaque buildup in the arteries. Test-tube studies have also found that compounds in radicchio may help attack cancer cells. While more human research is needed, adding more chicories to your diet appears to be beneficial.

Those on blood-thinning medications should avoid drastically increasing consumption of chicory vegetables, since many of them are high in vitamin K (see page 35).

[SEA VEGETABLES]

– ALGAE ANTIOXIDANTS –

Sea vegetables include edible seaweeds and algae, such as nori, dulse, kombu, wakame, spirulina, and chlorella. They offer many nutrients that soothe inflammation. While each kind of seaweed has a unique nutritional profile, they're all good sources of antioxidants, the essential mineral iodine, and dietary fiber. Seaweeds are also a source of anti-inflammatory omega-3 fatty acids.

Choosing Sea Vegetables

Seaweed is often sold as packages of dehydrated sheets and can be found at Asian markets, health food stores, the international aisle of some grocery stores, and online retailers. Chlorella and spirulina are most commonly available in powdered forms.

In the Kitchen

Seaweeds have a briny, umami taste. Dried seaweed has many culinary uses, and can be rehydrated by soaking dried sheets in water for 5 to 10 minutes. Freeze-dried seaweed has higher levels of nutrients than sun-dried and oven-dried seaweed.

HOW TO EAT MORE

- *Crumble dried seaweed and sprinkle over salad dressings or popcorn*
- *Make a salad with rehydrated seaweed tossed in a dressing of sesame oil, rice vinegar, honey, ginger, and tamari or soy sauce*

DID YOU KNOW?

NASA scientists are researching the potential of spirulina to grow in space, as it is considered an excellent source of nutrients for astronauts.

NUTRITION PER
5 GRAMS OF DRIED SEAWEED SNACKS*

Calories	60
Fat	4 g
Protein	3 g
Carbohydrates	2 g
Fiber	2 g
Natural sugars	0 g
Sodium	100 mg
Potassium	180 mg

*Nutrition varies based on brand, type of seaweed, and preparation methods

SEA VEGETABLES AND YOUR DIET

Sea vegetables are generally a safe and healthy addition to most diets. Chlorella and spirulina contain all of the essential amino acids and are complete protein sources, making them a good protein option for vegans and vegetarians.

Some varieties contain dangerously high levels of iodine and can increase the risk of iodine toxicity when consumed in excess. Getting too much iodine can interfere with normal thyroid function. Consume seaweed in moderation, and if you have thyroid issues, speak with your doctor before trying seaweed.

Seaweeds may also absorb heavy metals, such as mercury and lead. While the amounts of heavy metals in seaweed are usually below dangerous levels, it's possible that they can build up in your body if you eat large amounts of seaweed. Organic seaweeds tend to have lower levels of heavy metals than nonorganic varieties.

[WHEATGRASS]

– FULL OF CHLOROPHYLL –

This young grass sprouts from the seeds of the wheat plant. It resembles straw, but has a green color. Touted as a superfood, wheatgrass is often consumed in juice form. Its therapeutic benefits are not well researched, yet preliminary studies suggest it has anti-inflammatory potential. It is rich in antioxidants, chlorophyll, fiber, and other compounds that fight inflammation.

Choosing Wheatgrass

Wheatgrass has a pungent, earthy flavor. It can be difficult to find fresh, but may be available at health food stores. More often, these stores carry bottled wheatgrass juice, powders, or tablets. When choosing a wheatgrass powder, look for one that just contains dried wheatgrass juice and does not have added sugar or unnecessary additives.

In the Kitchen

Both fresh wheatgrass and dried powders offer beneficial nutrients. It's not clear if any one preparation of wheatgrass has more anti-inflammatory properties than others.

HOW TO EAT MORE

- *Use fresh or powdered wheatgrass in homemade juices or smoothies*
- *Stir into pineapple, orange, or apple juice for a more pleasant taste*

DID YOU KNOW?

One small study found drinking wheatgrass juice daily for one month reduced symptoms and disease severity in individuals with ulcerative colitis.

NUTRITION PER
1 TABLESPOON OF
WHEATGRASS POWDER

Calories	25
Fat	0 g
Protein	1 g
Carbohydrates	6 g
Fiber	4 g
Natural sugars	0 g
Sodium	0 mg
Potassium	240 mg

WHEATGRASS AND YOUR DIET

To reap the benefits of wheatgrass, use it mindfully and in moderation. If you use wheatgrass supplements, keep in mind that supplements are not well regulated. Thus, they may contain different amounts of wheatgrass than listed, or may be contaminated.

Those with celiac disease or gluten sensitivity are advised to exercise caution when consuming wheatgrass. Wheatgrass is usually gluten-free, since it comes from a part of the plant that doesn't contain gluten. However, look for certified gluten-free brands to ensure that wheatgrass does not contain trace amounts of gluten.

Fresh wheatgrass, especially homegrown varieties, is susceptible to mold and bacteria. Due to the risk of contamination, pregnant or lactating women, children, and individuals with compromised immune systems should avoid wheatgrass.

[PEPPERS]

- VEGGIES WITH A CAPSAICIN KICK -

All peppers offer anti-inflammatory properties, despite their differences in taste and appearance. Bell peppers are rich in vitamin C and antioxidant pigments that give them their color. Hot peppers also contain the compound capsaicin, which is responsible for their spicy kick and has inflammation-fighting capabilities.

Choosing Peppers

Fresh peppers should have firm, smooth, and bright skin without wrinkles, and the stems should have no discoloration. For a mild, sweet taste, choose bell peppers. For a spicier kick, choose jalapeño, serrano, cayenne, or chili peppers.

In the Kitchen

Red bell peppers have more beta-carotene and vitamin C than green bell peppers, while hot peppers are the best sources of capsaicin. To preserve the antioxidants in peppers, eat them raw or cook them for short periods of time. Some cooking methods, such as stir-frying, microwaving, and steaming, can increase the antioxidant potential of peppers.

HOW TO EAT MORE

- *Stuff bell peppers with beans and whole grains*
- *Use seasonings made from dried peppers, such as red pepper flakes, cayenne pepper, and paprika*
- *Add chopped jalapeño or serrano pepper to salsas*

DID YOU KNOW?

Some say that green peppers are just unripe red ones. But this isn't always the case. The final color of a bell pepper depends on the type of seed used.

NUTRITION PER
1 MEDIUM RAW BELL PEPPER

Calories	37
Fat	0.4 g
Protein	1.2 g
Carbohydrates	7 g
Fiber	2.5 g
Natural sugars	5 g
Sodium	5 mg
Potassium	251 mg

PEPPERS AND YOUR DIET

Peppers are not a good choice for everyone. Some individuals with Crohn's disease or ulcerative colitis report a worsening of their symptoms after eating hot peppers.

Individuals with autoimmune or inflammatory conditions such as arthritis, psoriasis, lupus, or IBD are sometimes advised to avoid peppers. Peppers are part of the nightshade family, which contains compounds known as alkaloids that are thought to trigger inflammation. However, there is limited research (and no large-scale study) to support this idea. In fact, nightshade vegetables are full of nutrients and compounds that can actually help suppress inflammation.

If you have an inflammatory condition, a registered dietitian can help you identify foods that may be problematic for you and sort through any confusion about peppers and nightshades.

[TOMATOES]

– LYCOPENE-LOADED FRUITS –

Tomatoes have long been hailed as anti-inflammatory powerhouses. Their red color comes from the carotenoid pigment lycopene, which may help mitigate inflammatory processes in the body. Lycopene and other beneficial compounds in tomatoes may work together to reduce the risk of diseases associated with chronic inflammation.

Choosing Tomatoes

Tomatoes are in season during the late summer and early fall, but they can be enjoyed all year round. Choose tomatoes that are bright in color and free from cracks or bruises on their skin. Canned and jarred tomatoes and tomato products are highly nutritious, shelf-stable options.

In the Kitchen

Cooking tomatoes enhances their anti-inflammatory capacity, even if it does decrease their vitamin C content. Heat transforms lycopene into a more available form, while adding a source of fat (such as olive oil) during cooking also makes lycopene more absorbable. Canned tomatoes, tomato sauces, and tomato pastes are often higher in lycopene than fresh tomatoes.

HOW TO EAT MORE

- *Roast cherry tomatoes on the vine with olive oil and fresh herbs*
- *Serve fresh tomato slices with olive oil, balsamic vinegar, and basil*
- *Stir tomato paste into soups and stews*

DID YOU KNOW?

The lycopene content of tomatoes increases as they ripen on the vine, and the skin of tomatoes is rich in nutrients.

NUTRITION PER
1 MEDIUM RAW TOMATO

Calories	22
Fat	0.2 g
Protein	1.1 g
Carbohydrates	4.8 g
Fiber	1.5 g
Natural sugars	3.2 g
Sodium	6 mg
Potassium	292 mg

TOMATOES AND YOUR DIET

Tomatoes are gluten-free, vegan, vegetarian, and low-carb and can fit into many eating patterns, with some caveats. Those who need to watch their potassium intake due to kidney disease or other conditions may need to limit their consumption of tomatoes. Tomato pastes, juices, and sauces are more concentrated and higher in potassium than fresh tomatoes. Tomatoes and tomato products may also trigger symptoms of acid reflux and heartburn.

Like peppers, tomatoes are a member of the nightshade family and are sometimes accused of triggering inflammation in those with autoimmune or inflammatory conditions. However, tomatoes are highly nutritious and full of nutrients that may help fight inflammation. Speak with a registered dietitian if you have an inflammatory condition and wonder if nightshades contribute to your symptoms.

[AVOCADOS]

– THE HEALTHY FAT HEROES –

Avocados are worthy of their hype. These creamy fruits are packed with nutrients and compounds that can suppress the body's inflammatory response. They are rich in heart-healthy monounsaturated fats, carotenoids, and vitamin E. Plus, avocados are an excellent source of dietary fiber that supports a healthy gut.

Choosing Avocados

To test if an avocado is ripe, press your thumb into the skin. Avocados that are ready to eat should feel soft but not mushy to the touch. Ripe avocados may also have darker skin compared to unripe ones, but this depends on the variety.

In the Kitchen

The healthy fats in avocado help you absorb the fat-soluble nutrients and compounds it contains. Adding avocado to a meal may even help offset the effect of foods that contribute to inflammation. One study found that those who ate a hamburger with avocado slices had lower levels of inflammatory markers than those who consumed a plain hamburger.

HOW TO EAT MORE

- *Mash avocado and mix it with red onion, garlic, tomatoes, cilantro, and lime juice*
- *Swap mayo or sour cream with puréed avocado*
- *For a smoothie, blend avocado with leafy greens, frozen mango, lime juice, and water*

DID YOU KNOW?

Avocado oil also has anti-inflammatory properties and contains the same healthy fats, antioxidants, and vitamins as the fruit.

NUTRITION PER
1 CUP SLICED, RAW AVOCADO

Calories	234
Fat	21 g
Protein	2.9 g
Carbohydrates	12 g
Fiber	10 g
Natural sugars	1 g
Sodium	10 mg
Potassium	708 mg

AVOCADOS AND YOUR DIET

Rich in monounsaturated fats, fiber, and potassium, avocados are a healthy addition to meals for those with heart disease. Plus, they can fit into nearly every special diet. They are an excellent source of healthy fat for low-carb or keto eating plans. Those with diabetes can enjoy avocados with little effect on blood sugar levels. Thanks to its creamy texture, avocado can be used as a plant-based substitution for mayo, butter, yogurt, or sour cream on vegan diets.

Since avocados contain a decent amount of vitamin K, individuals on blood-thinning medications should watch their avocado consumption and keep vitamin K intake consistent (see page 35). Those who need to be mindful of how much potassium they consume, such as individuals with kidney disease, should be cautious about overeating avocados.

[BERRIES]

– FREE RADICAL FIGHTING FRUITS –

Berries make up an incredibly nutritious group of fruits that can tone down inflammation, due to their high content of vitamin C, anthocyanins, and several other polyphenol compounds. They help protect against free radical damage to cells and organs and suppress inflammatory signals. Some varieties of berries, such as raspberries, are exceptionally high in dietary fiber, which helps maintain a healthy gut populated with bacteria that partake in the body's inflammatory defenses.

All berries have anti-inflammatory potential. Lesser known varieties, including huckleberries, lingonberries, and boysenberries, offer considerable inflammation-fighting benefits. In fact, wild huckleberries and lingonberries have some of the highest antioxidant capacities out of all berries, according to a measure known as the oxygen radical absorption capacity (ORAC).

Choosing Berries

Look for berries that are dry and plump with smooth skin that's void of bruises, wrinkles, or dark spots. Avoid washing berries until just before using to prevent them from going bad too quickly. The freshest berries are typically available in the summer months. For longer-lasting options that are accessible all year, opt for frozen or dried berries.

In the Kitchen

Raw, frozen, dried, and cooked berries all offer benefits. Cooking berries may reduce the levels of some nutrients and compounds but increase the amounts of others. Adding sugar to cooked berries, such as when making jellies, can dilute their nutritional value.

Frozen berries are just as nutritious as fresh ones. When it comes to dried berries, opt for freeze-dried if you can, as these tend to retain more nutrients than dehydrated varieties.

NUTRITION PER
1 CUP RAW RASPBERRIES

Calories	65
Fat	0.8 g
Protein	1.5 g
Carbohydrates	15 g
Fiber	8 g
Natural sugars	5 g
Sodium	1 mg
Potassium	186 mg

HOW TO EAT MORE

- *Combine freeze-dried strawberries with nuts for a snack*
- *Blend frozen strawberries with cooked beets, banana, and almond butter for a smoothie*
- *Pulse fresh cranberries in a food processor with jalapeños, green onions, cilantro, and lime juice for a fun twist on salsa*
- *Enjoy berries on their own, on top of Greek or plant-based yogurt, and mixed into granola or oatmeal*

BERRIES AND YOUR DIET

Berries are vegan, vegetarian, and gluten-free. Since they are lower in carbohydrates than many other fruits, berries can be enjoyed in moderation on low-carb and keto diets.

Eating more berries may help boost heart and brain health and reduce the risk of diseases related to chronic inflammation. However, it's best to limit consumption of products and foods made with berries that contain a lot of added sugar. Sweetened juices, jellies, sauces, and desserts may seem like a good source of berries but can sometimes be loaded with sugar and other unhealthy ingredients.

Cranberries, and cranberry juice in particular, are often recommended to prevent and treat urinary tract infections (UTIs). However, studies on this topic offer conflicting results. If you have frequent UTIs, consult with your health care provider about using cranberry juice or supplements to see if they would be beneficial for you.

VARIETIES TO TRY

- *Raspberries: A balanced blend of sweet and tart flavors, perfect for a snack*
- *Blueberries: Eat them by the handful during their peak season—summer*
- *Strawberries: Use these mild, sweet berries in a savory dish to switch it up*
- *Huckleberries: Huckleberries have a sweet taste similar to blueberries*
- *Goji berries: Add these slightly sour and tart dried berries to your morning oatmeal*
- *Lingonberries: These have a tart and slightly sour flavor*
- *Blackberries: Let them ripen fully for the sweetest taste and juiciest texture*
- *Cranberries: Capitalize on fresh cranberries when they're in season in the fall and add to sauces, salsas, and grain dishes*
- *Elderberries: Their earthy, sweet-tart flavor makes them a good companion to sweeter berries and grapes, but make sure to cook them first*

DID YOU KNOW?

Wild varieties of some berries, such as blueberries, are higher in antioxidants than ordinary berries. They can be found in the freezer section of many grocery and health food stores.

Opposite, clockwise from top: Strawberries bring summer sweetness to a milkshake; serve berries with granola and yogurt for a winning anti-inflammatory combo; fresh cranberries will add a tart twist to salsas and salads.

[CHERRIES]

– RICH IN ANTHOCYANINS –

The deep red and purple pigments found in cherries, known as anthocyanins, have anti-inflammatory and antioxidant properties. Some of the research-backed benefits of cherries include improving symptoms of arthritis and gout, decreasing blood levels of inflammatory markers, and boosting exercise recovery.

Choosing Cherries

Cherries are available in tart/sour (bright red) and sweet (dark red) varieties. Look for in-season fruits during the summer months, and choose ones that are firm with smooth, shiny skin that's free from bruises.

In the Kitchen

Since anthocyanins are sensitive to heat and light, fresh or frozen cherries will likely give you more of an anti-inflammatory boost than cooked cherries. When it comes to dried cherries and cherry juice, some studies suggest that, fortunately, the polyphenol content and activity of these preparations is similar to that of raw cherries.

HOW TO EAT MORE

- *Make a fruit salsa with chopped cherries, red onion, mint, and lemon juice, and serve over fish*
- *Blend frozen cherries with banana, almond milk, and almond butter for a smoothie*
- *Enjoy cherries on their own or on top of oatmeal, chia pudding, or yogurt*

DID YOU KNOW?

Due to their higher anthocyanin content, tart cherries may be more effective at relieving muscle pain than sweet cherries.

NUTRITION PER
1 CUP RAW CHERRIES

Calories	95
Fat	0.3 g
Protein	1.6 g
Carbohydrates	24 g
Fiber	3.2 g
Natural sugars	9.2 g
Sodium	0 mg
Potassium	333 mg

CHERRIES AND YOUR DIET

Cherries are suitable for vegetarian, vegan, and gluten-free diets and may fit into keto meal plans in small amounts. They are a healthy source of complex carbohydrates for those with diabetes.

If you are following an anti-inflammatory diet to help with symptoms of arthritis or gout, cherries may be an especially beneficial addition to your meals. Some research suggests that eating cherries can reduce gout attacks, especially in combination with the anti-gout medication allopurinol. Cherries may help by lowering blood levels of uric acid, which builds up in the body and crystallizes around the joints.

Cherries are also recommended for athletes, especially as tart cherry juice. They may help reduce pain, decrease inflammatory markers in the body, and enhance recovery after exercise.

[GRAPES]

Grapes—red, purple, and green—are rich in antioxidants and other compounds that shield cells and tissues from damage and inflammation. Red and purple grapes contain anthocyanins, while all types of grapes have resveratrol, a beneficial compound, associated with red wine, which may protect against diseases related to chronic inflammation and promote longevity.

Choosing Grapes

Grapes should be plump and firm with no apparent bruises or dark spots. Fresh bunches should be tightly packed together. Red and purple grapes are usually sweeter than green grapes, which can be slightly sour. Remove portions from a bunch of grapes by cutting the stem with scissors, instead of plucking off individual grapes, to keep the stem from drying out.

In the Kitchen

Raw grapes retain fractionally more anti-inflammatory nutrients than cooked ones. Keep the skin on, since it is highly concentrated with beneficial compounds.

HOW TO EAT MORE

- *Freeze grapes to enjoy as a cold treat or to blend into a slushie*
- *Cook grapes down to use as an oatmeal topping*
- *Roast grapes and use them as a salad topping or as part of a roasted vegetable medley*

DID YOU KNOW?

Green "Cotton candy" grapes do not taste tart but have a sweet flavor that resembles the town fair treat from which they get their name.

NUTRITION PER
1 CUP RAW GRAPES

Calories	62
Fat	0.3 g
Protein	0.6 g
Carbohydrates	16 g
Fiber	0.8 g
Natural Sugars	15 g
Sodium	2 mg
Potassium	176 mg

GRAPES AND YOUR DIET

Grapes are a wonderful addition to almost any diet. Even though they contain natural sugar, they're considered a diabetes-friendly fruit. Thanks to their low glycemic index—a measure of how much a food increases blood sugar—grapes do not appear to raise blood sugar when consumed in moderation.

One of the most commonly consumed forms of this fruit is wine. Some studies have found a link between red wine consumption and a lower risk of heart disease or heart attacks, possibly due to the resveratrol in wine. However, research remains inconclusive. Enjoying red wine in moderation—up to one glass per day for women and two glasses per day for men—may be a good choice for those who already drink alcohol. On the other hand, excess alcohol intake contributes to inflammation and can increase the risk of a number of health problems. It's also unclear if red wine is beneficial to those who do not already drink alcohol.

[PINEAPPLE]

– BROMELAIN BOOSTER –

Just one cup of chopped pineapple provides over 100% of the Daily Value (DV) for vitamin C, a water-soluble nutrient that acts as an antioxidant in the body. It also contains bromelain, a group of enzymes that may help reduce inflammatory markers and stimulate the release of compounds that fight inflammation.

Choosing Pineapple

Both whole and sliced fresh pineapple are often available at grocery stores. To choose a ripe whole pineapple, look for one that is slightly soft when pressed. When selecting pre-cut pineapple, make sure the slices are free of discoloration and mold. Refer to the "best by" date to choose a quantity that fits your timeline for using the fruit.

In the Kitchen

Eating pineapple raw or cooking it for short periods of time is the best way to maintain this fruit's anti-inflammatory nutrients. Both vitamin C and bromelain are heat sensitive.

HOW TO EAT MORE

- *Add sliced pineapple to yogurt or smoothies*
- *Serve a pineapple salsa on fish tacos*
- *Make a dessert of grilled pineapple rings brushed with olive oil, cinnamon, turmeric, and ginger*

DID YOU KNOW?

The enzymes in pineapple help break down protein and may improve digestion in individuals who do not make enough digestive enzymes, such as those with pancreatic insufficiency.

NUTRITION PER
1 CUP RAW PINEAPPLE CHUNKS

Calories	82
Fat	0.2 g
Protein	0.9 g
Carbohydrates	22 g
Fiber	2.3 g
Natural Sugars	16 g
Sodium	2 mg
Potassium	180 mg

PINEAPPLE AND YOUR DIET

Pineapple is naturally gluten-free, vegan, and vegetarian. It is full of nutrients but is relatively high in carbohydrates compared to some other fruits. Enjoy pineapple in moderation and in combination with foods that do not raise blood sugar if you have diabetes or are watching your carbohydrate intake.

Adding pineapple to your diet may be especially beneficial in some scenarios. Bromelain is claimed to help relieve joint pain associated with arthritis and reduce inflammation caused by surgery, intense exercise, and sports injuries. Several studies support these claims and have found that bromelain may be effective at suppressing inflammation.

However, pineapple is acidic and may trigger heartburn. Individuals with gastroesophageal reflux disease (GERD) may want to limit consumption.

[WATERMELON]

– CAROTENOID POWERHOUSE –

Like other red and pink plant foods, watermelon contains pigments that give it both a pretty color and inflammation-fighting powers. These include beta-carotene and lycopene, two carotenoids that down-regulate the inflammation process. Yellow watermelon also contains beta-cryptoxanthin, a provitamin A carotenoid that has been linked to a reduced risk of rheumatoid arthritis.

Choosing Watermelon

Choose watermelons that have smooth skin without cracks or cuts. Check the "field spot" to assess ripeness. The field spot is the area of a watermelon where it rested on the ground while on the vine. Watermelons with yellow field spots are riper and sweeter than those with white ones.

In the Kitchen

It's often claimed that fruit loses nutrients after being cut. Interestingly, the vitamin C and carotenoid content of watermelon does not appear to degrade after it is sliced and is mostly maintained even after several days in the refrigerator.

HOW TO EAT MORE

- *Blend watermelon with lime juice and ground cinnamon, pour into popsicle molds, and freeze*
- *Make a salad with watermelon, arugula, red onion, feta cheese, lime juice, and mint*

DID YOU KNOW?

All parts of a watermelon are edible! Watermelon rind can be eaten raw, pickled, or cooked. It contains the amino acid citrulline, which has been linked to lower blood pressure and other benefits.

NUTRITION PER
1 CUP DICED, RAW WATERMELON

Calories	46
Fat	0.2 g
Protein	0.9 g
Carbohydrates	11 g
Fiber	0.6 g
Natural Sugars	9 g
Sodium	2 mg
Potassium	170 mg

WATERMELON AND YOUR DIET

This juicy fruit is naturally vegan, vegetarian, and gluten-free. As its name suggests, watermelon is over 90% water. The high water content of this fruit makes it a very filling option that's low in calories and carbohydrates. Eating watermelon can also help keep you hydrated, which aids the body's anti-inflammatory response (see page 17).

Watermelon makes a delicious addition to most special diets and can be incorporated into eating plans for certain health conditions. Compounds in watermelon may help lower blood pressure in those with hypertension. Watermelon is also a good fruit choice for those with diabetes. To maintain good blood sugar control, enjoy watermelon in moderation with other foods that contain protein, healthy fats, and fiber.

[CITRUS]

– VITAMIN C BOOSTERS –

Chock full of the antioxidant vitamin C, all citrus fruits count as anti-inflammatory foods. Oranges, grapefruits, lemons, and limes contain beneficial compounds that help quell inflammation and protect cells from underlying damage that contributes to disease. Beta-cryptoxanthin is found in oranges, while grapefruit is a source of lycopene and beta-carotene.

Choosing Citrus

Ripe citrus feels heavy for its size and has firm skin that's void of bruises or soft spots. Check citrus for spots of white mold on the skin before purchasing or eating. For the freshest, juiciest, and sweetest citrus, enjoy these fruits in peak season during the winter.

In the Kitchen

Since vitamin C can degrade at high temperatures, it's best to eat citrus fruits raw or use cooking techniques that expose them to heat for only short periods of time. Citrus peels are edible and also contain anti-inflammatory nutrients, but they can have a bitter taste and are difficult to digest.

HOW TO EAT MORE

• Use freshly squeezed lemon or lime juice for dressings and marinades, or add it to water

• Brush grapefruit halves with olive oil and honey, sprinkle with cinnamon, and broil for 3 minutes

DID YOU KNOW? *Citrus fruits contain citrate, which is thought to help prevent kidney stones from forming.*

NUTRITION PER
1 LARGE RAW ORANGE

Calories	87
Fat	0.2 g
Protein	1.7 g
Carbohydrates	22 g
Fiber	4.4 g
Natural Sugars	17 g
Sodium	0 mg
Potassium	333 mg

CITRUS AND YOUR DIET

All citrus is vegan, vegetarian, and gluten-free. The flesh and juice of oranges and grapefruits are consumed, while only the juice of lemons and limes is typically used. Plus, the typical portions of oranges and grapefruit are bigger and higher in carbohydrates than small servings of lemon or lime juice. Thus, they may not fit into keto or very low-carb eating plans. Since orange and grapefruit juices are more concentrated in carbohydrates and lower in fiber than whole fruits, those with diabetes may want to limit juice consumption and choose whole fruits instead.

Grapefruit and grapefruit juice can interact with how the body metabolizes medications, including some statin drugs, blood pressure medications, oral contraceptives, and immunosuppressant drugs. If you take medications, check with your doctor or pharmacist about possible interactions with grapefruit.

[POMEGRANATE]

– ANTI-AGING ARILS –

Pomegranate has potent anti-inflammatory properties. Filled with polyphenols and vitamin C, it is abundant in antioxidants that inhibit free radical damage to tissues and have anti-aging effects. Increasing evidence suggests that pomegranate juice may help calm inflammation associated with heart disease, IBD, and arthritis.

Choosing Pomegranate

Grocery stores often carry several forms of pomegranates, including whole fruits, containers of arils (the small, juicy sacs), and bottles of juice. The best-quality pomegranates have a bright, ruby red rind and firm, smooth skin. When choosing arils or juice, check the "best by" date to ensure you're purchasing a product that won't spoil right away.

In the Kitchen

Pomegranate juice is more concentrated compared to pomegranate arils but may have lower amounts of some nutrients, such as vitamin C.

HOW TO EAT MORE

- *Add arils to salads, yogurt, and oatmeal, or sprinkle them on fish*
- *Use pomegranate juice in smoothies*
- *Mix pomegranate juice with seltzer water for a refreshing beverage*

DID YOU KNOW?

Pomegranate juice contains three times more antioxidants than green tea and red wine.

NUTRITION PER
1/2 CUP RAW ARILS

Calories	72
Fat	1 g
Protein	1.5 g
Carbohydrates	16 g
Fiber	3.5 g
Natural Sugars	12 g
Sodium	3 mg
Potassium	205 mg

POMEGRANATE AND YOUR DIET

Pomegranate arils contain many nutrients and are a good source of fiber. Plus, they suit vegan, vegetarian, gluten-free, heart-healthy, and diabetes-friendly eating patterns.

Pomegranate juice does not contain fiber and is fairly high in carbohydrates, mostly from natural sugars. Those with diabetes can consume pomegranate juice in moderation and alongside foods that contain protein and healthy fats. Making a smoothie with pomegranate juice, frozen berries, Greek yogurt, and chia seeds is a good way to reap the benefits of pomegranates without spiking blood sugar. If using store-bought juice, check the label to make sure it is 100% juice with no added sugar.

If you take statins or blood pressure medications, discuss with your health care provider before drinking pomegranate juice, as it may interact with the metabolism of some drugs.

[CANTALOUPE]

– CAROTENOID-RICH FRUIT –

Cantaloupe is rich in micronutrients that act as antioxidants, especially vitamins A and C. One cup of cantaloupe provides over 100% of the DV for vitamin A in the form of the carotenoid beta-carotene. Eating carotenoid-rich fruits, such as cantaloupe, has been linked to decreased markers of inflammation in the blood.

Choosing Cantaloupe

Choose cantaloupes that have a beige rind with raised ridges on the surface. Similar to watermelon (see page 77), ripe cantaloupes have a yellow "field spot." They should have a sweet smell, firm skin that gives a little when pressed, and no soft spots.

In the Kitchen

Keep cantaloupe raw to preserve vitamin C. Not much is known about the effects of cooking methods on other nutrients in cantaloupe, but a short cooking time likely has minimal impact on levels of beneficial nutrients and compounds.

HOW TO EAT MORE

• *Eat freshly chopped cantaloupe as a snack*

• *Add cantaloupe balls to salads*

• *Make a chilled soup, blending chopped cantaloupe with orange and lemon juices, cinnamon, honey, and fresh mint*

DID YOU KNOW?

Honeydew melon also offers anti-inflammatory benefits. Though it lacks beta-carotene, it provides vitamin C, dietary fiber, and other carotenoids such as lutein and zeaxanthin.

NUTRITION PER
1 CUP DICED, RAW CANTALOUPE

Calories	53
Fat	0.3 g
Protein	1.3 g
Carbohydrates	13 g
Fiber	1.4 g
Natural Sugars	12 g
Sodium	25 mg
Potassium	417 mg

CANTALOUPE AND YOUR DIET

Cantaloupe is naturally vegetarian, vegan, and gluten-free but may not fit into very low-carb or keto diets. Though it contains natural sugars, it also provides fiber that can help those with diabetes maintain good blood sugar control. Cantaloupe is a good source of potassium, which is a helpful nutrient for those with high blood pressure, but may need to be limited in individuals with kidney disease.

The netted skin of cantaloupes can trap bacteria that cause foodborne illnesses, which can be especially problematic for older adults, pregnant women, and those with compromised immune systems. When preparing cantaloupes, prevent transferring bacteria from the skin to the flesh. Rinse and scrub cantaloupe with a vegetable brush under running water before slicing. After it has been cut, store cantaloupe in the refrigerator for up to a couple days. Do not eat cantaloupe that has been at room temperature for longer than 2 hours.

[KIWI]

– KISSPER-RICH FRUIT –

Kiwis pack a ton of nutrients and compounds that fight oxidative damage and balance out free radicals that contribute to inflammation. They're excellent sources of vitamin C and contain a variety of other antioxidants. A unique peptide found in kiwis, known as kissper, is being explored for its anti-inflammatory effects.

Choosing Kiwis

You can tell a kiwi is ripe if it has brown, fuzzy skin with no bruises and yields when you gently press your thumb into it. Ripe kiwis also have a sweet fragrance, indicative of their sweet flavor profile that combines tastes of strawberry, pineapple, and banana.

In the Kitchen

Similar to other vitamin C-rich fruits, kiwis should be enjoyed raw to maintain maximum levels of this nutrient. Golden kiwis, which have yellow flesh, have even more vitamin C than their green counterparts.

HOW TO EAT MORE

- *Slice a kiwi in half and scoop out the flesh with a spoon as a snack*
- *Peel and slice kiwis, then add to a fruit salad with grapes and pineapple*
- *Make a yogurt parfait with sliced kiwi (see page 142)*

NUTRITION PER
1 RAW KIWI

Calories	42
Fat	0.4 g
Protein	0.8 g
Carbohydrates	10 g
Fiber	2.1 g
Natural Sugars	6 g
Sodium	2 mg
Potassium	215 mg

KIWI AND YOUR DIET

Kiwi may not be as popular as other fruits, but it's a delicious addition to anti-inflammatory eating plans nonetheless. You can enjoy kiwi on vegan, vegetarian, and gluten-free diets. It has fewer carbohydrates than some other fruits, packs a good amount of dietary fiber, and can fit into keto and low-carb diets.

For those with heart disease, high blood pressure, or diabetes, kiwi offers many beneficial nutrients, including potassium and fiber. This healthy fruit also contains compounds that may help soothe inflammation associated with IBD. Furthermore, individuals who follow a low-FODMAP diet to improve symptoms of IBS can enjoy kiwi, as it is considered a low-FODMAP fruit.

DID YOU KNOW? *Kiwi's anti-inflammatory potential has led to its use in homemade face masks. Anecdotal accounts claim that applying mashed kiwi to the face soothes acne breakouts and inflamed areas.*

[APPLES]

- POLYPHENOLIC PROTECTOR -

The age-old saying "an apple a day keeps the doctor away" is telling of the anti-inflammatory potential of this crunchy fruit. Eating apples on a regular basis has been linked to lower blood levels of inflammatory markers, including C-reactive protein (CRP). Plus, apples contain polyphenols and fiber that may support healthy gut bacteria that influence inflammation processes.

Choosing Apples

Look for apples that are firm and smooth with no bruises or soft spots. Apples range from sweet to tart. They tend to be the freshest and most flavorful during their peak season of September through October. Fuji and Honeycrisp varieties are quite sweet, while Granny Smith apples are the tartest.

In the Kitchen

Raw apples contain more vitamin C and beneficial compounds than cooked ones. To preserve polyphenols, keep the skins on apples when cooking them. The skin is also the primary source of fiber.

HOW TO EAT MORE

- *Spread nut butter on apple slices for a snack*
- *Add apple slices to salads and grate apples into slaws*
- *Bake whole apples in their skins for dessert*

DID YOU KNOW?

Apples maintain their polyphenol content during storage. Even after several weeks in storage, the levels of polyphenols and antioxidant activity in apples are similar to those at harvest.

NUTRITION PER
1 MEDIUM RAW APPLE WITH ITS SKIN

Calories	95
Fat	0.3 g
Protein	0.5 g
Carbohydrates	25 g
Fiber	4.4 g
Natural Sugars	19 g
Sodium	2 mg
Potassium	195 mg

APPLES AND YOUR DIET

Eating an apple every day may not literally stop you from getting sick, but it can support your body's defense against chronic inflammation. Apples can be enjoyed as part of many special eating styles, including vegan, vegetarian, and gluten-free diets. Due to their carbohydrate content, apples are usually limited on keto and very low-carb diets.

For those with diabetes or blood sugar regulation issues, apples prove to be a suitable choice. They have a fairly low glycemic index and are high in fiber. This means they are unlikely to lead to rapid spikes in blood sugar. However, apple juice and cider can spike blood sugar, as they do not contain the fiber found in whole apples that slows down the digestion of sugar. Some juices and ciders may also contain added sugar. It's best to limit their consumption.

[OATS]

Oats are mini powerhouses of antioxidants, namely avenanthramides and ferulic acid. Not only do these compounds help protect against free radical damage, they may fight inflammation by stopping the release of pro-inflammatory cytokines in the body, among other mechanisms. Oats also contain selenium, an essential mineral with antioxidant properties.

Choosing Oats

Oats come in many different varieties. Instant and old-fashioned rolled oats are more processed and have shorter cook times than steel-cut oats, but all types are highly nutritious. When selecting oats, check the ingredient list to ensure there are no added sugars or artificial flavorings.

In the Kitchen

You can enjoy raw oats, but soaked and cooked oats tend to be easier to digest and may be more beneficial. Soaking or cooking helps to release some of the anti-inflammatory nutrients in oats, making them easier to absorb.

HOW TO EAT MORE

• Make overnight oats by soaking one part oats with one part milk; stir in seeds, nuts, and fruit
• Combine oats with cranberries and pumpkin seeds in healthy snack bars (see page 156).

DID YOU KNOW?

Ground oats are a great substitution for flour and can boost the nutrition of your baked goods. You can swap oat flour for all-purpose flour in most recipes!

NUTRITION PER
1 CUP COOKED OATMEAL

Calories	158
Fat	3.2 g
Protein	6 g
Carbohydrates	27 g
Fiber	4 g
Natural Sugars	1.1 g
Sodium	115 mg
Potassium	143 mg

OATS AND YOUR DIET

Oats are naturally vegan, vegetarian, low-sodium, and gluten-free. However, oats may be contaminated with gluten-containing grains during storage or processing. If you have celiac disease or gluten sensitivity, be sure to purchase oats that are certified gluten-free. Oats are not suitable on some special diets, such as the keto diet.

In addition to antioxidants, oats are a great source of beta-glucan fiber. This soluble fiber may help lower cholesterol and reduce your risk of heart disease. It's also been shown to improve insulin sensitivity and blood sugar control in those with diabetes.

Cooked oats are full of fiber that can help keep you regular and relieve constipation, but raw oats may trigger digestive discomfort. Soaking oats in liquid or softening them with the addition of other ingredients can make raw oats easier to digest.

[QUINOA]

– PREBIOTIC BOOSTER –

Quinoa, a seed that's cooked and eaten like a grain, is loaded with nutrients and compounds that may help soothe inflammation. It's high in fiber that acts as a prebiotic in the gut, nourishing healthy bacteria and promoting the production of short-chain fatty acids that regulate anti-inflammatory mechanisms.

Choosing Quinoa

You can find quinoa by other whole grains at the grocery store. It's available in many different colors, including white, yellow, red, black, and tricolor. All kinds have a nutty, earthy taste, but red and black quinoa tends to have a stronger flavor than white.

In the Kitchen

For a more robust antioxidant content, choose red, black, or yellow quinoa over white. These varieties get their colors from betalain pigments that act as antioxidants. Unlike most other grains, quinoa has a short cooking time (12 to 15 minutes). Rinse and drain quinoa in a sieve before cooking to remove the bitter coating that develops on the seeds.

HOW TO EAT MORE

- *Cook quinoa with vegetable broth and seasonings for more flavor, and serve with fish and vegetables*
- *Turn quinoa into breakfast and serve with fruit, cinnamon, and pecans*

DID YOU KNOW?

Experts believe that quinoa can be part of the solution to world hunger, thanks to its adaptability to growing conditions and excellent nutritional profile.

NUTRITION PER
1 CUP COOKED QUINOA

Calories	222
Fat	3.6 g
Protein	8 g
Carbohydrates	39 g
Fiber	5 g
Natural Sugars	1.6 g
Sodium	13 mg
Potassium	318 mg

QUINOA AND YOUR DIET

Quinoa is an excellent addition to many special diets. It is naturally gluten-free and safe for those with celiac disease and gluten sensitivity. Due to the possibility of exposure to other grains during processing, be sure to purchase certified gluten-free quinoa.

Those who follow a vegetarian or vegan diet may benefit from adding quinoa to their meals. Quinoa is relatively high in protein compared to other grains. Even more, it is considered a complete, high-quality protein that provides all of the essential amino acids.

Individuals with diabetes can also enjoy quinoa in moderate portions. Though it contains carbohydrates, it provides fiber, protein, and fat and thus has a minimal effect on blood sugar. However, quinoa is too high in carbohydrates to fit into a keto diet.

[RICE]

Rice, particularly brown, black, red, and wild varieties, has several nutrients and inflammation-busting compounds. Compared to white rice, which has the husk, bran, and germ removed, these varieties have the nutrient-rich bran and germ intact. They provide fiber and contain an array of antioxidants that shield cells from free radical damage that leads to inflammation.

Choosing Rice

Grocery stores offer several kinds of rice. When cooked, short-grain rice is softer and stickier than medium- and long-grain varieties, which have less starch and come out fluffier. Most types of rice have a mild, nutty taste, and wild rice tends to have a stronger and earthier flavor than other types.

In the Kitchen

Choose brown, black, red, or wild rice over white rice for more nutrients and fiber. Cooking leads to some nutrient loss, but certain cooking methods do not appear to be better than others.

HOW TO EAT MORE

- *Serve rice as a side dish, add it to salads, or use it in soups*
- *Make a grain bowl with brown rice, tofu, vegetables, and ginger-miso dressing*
- *Combine rice with bell peppers, jalapeños, corn, black beans, lime juice, and cilantro*

DID YOU KNOW?

Wild rice has 30 times the antioxidant activity of white rice and contains more fiber and protein.

NUTRITION PER
1 CUP COOKED BROWN RICE

Calories	216
Fat	1.8 g
Protein	5 g
Carbohydrates	45 g
Fiber	3.5 g
Natural Sugars	0.7 g
Sodium	10 mg
Potassium	84 mg

RICE AND YOUR DIET

Rice is gluten-free in its natural form. However, rice may be sold in blends with other grains or in pre-seasoned packets that have gluten-containing ingredients. If you follow a gluten-free diet, read the ingredient list to make sure your rice is completely free of gluten.

Some products with rice can be high in sodium or contain unhealthy oils and therefore may not be suitable for anti-inflammatory eating. Instead, opt for plain rice and add healthy seasonings of your own.

To maintain good blood sugar control, individuals with diabetes can incorporate rice in moderate portions alongside non-starchy vegetables and healthy proteins and fats. Brown, black, red, and wild rice are whole grains and have lower glycemic indexes than white rice.

[LEGUMES]

Legumes include beans, peas, and lentils, all of which are highly nutritious foodstuffs and provide compounds that help dampen inflammation in the body. Lentils, chickpeas, and beans, such as black, pinto, kidney, and white are full of many anti-inflammatory and antioxidant polyphenols. Peas contain some of the same nutrients and compounds as their fellow legumes. Plus, they're rich in vitamin C and beta-carotene, both antioxidants.

You may be familiar with the popular rhyme about beans being the magical "fruit" that makes you pass gas. The fiber in beans can keep you regular, but it also contributes to a legume's anti-inflammatory mechanisms. Fiber supports a healthy gut microbiome, which plays a role in regulating inflammation processes in the body.

Choosing Legumes

While legumes have fairly similar nutritional profiles, they differ in taste and texture. Pinto, black, and white beans have mild, earthy flavors and creamy consistencies. Lentils are smaller than most beans and have an earthy and slightly peppery taste, while chickpeas (garbanzo beans) have hints of nutty undertones and a grainier texture than other varieties.

Both dried and canned legumes are widely available. They are very affordable and can be stored for long periods of time. Before cooking dried beans, lentils, or peas, sort through them to find and remove broken, shriveled, or discolored ones.

NUTRITION PER
1 CUP BOILED LENTILS

Calories	230
Fat	0.8 g
Protein	18 g
Carbohydrates	40 g
Fiber	16 g
Natural Sugars	3.6 g
Sodium	4 mg
Potassium	731 mg

HOW TO EAT MORE

- Add beans to tacos, rice dishes, soups, pasta, and more
- Blend white beans with olive oil, garlic, lemon juice, and fresh herbs to make a creamy dip
- Roast chickpeas with olive oil and seasonings for a crunchy snack
- Stir black beans into salsa
- Make a smoothie with steamed green peas, frozen banana, almond milk, mint, and almond butter

In the Kitchen

Legumes should always be eaten cooked, as the cooking process makes them digestible and helps remove anti-nutrients that may reduce nutrient absorption. Soaking beans before cooking may improve their nutritional value. To soak dried legumes, place them in a bowl or container and cover with a couple inches of water. Let them sit for 8 to 12 hours, drain, and cook. To cut back on cooking time, prepare beans in a pressure cooker instead of on the stovetop.

Canned beans can be enjoyed right away, since they are always precooked. The canning process also decreases anti-nutrient levels. However, some canned beans are high in sodium. If you are watching your sodium intake, purchase low-sodium or no-added-salt beans. Rinsing beans before eating can reduce their sodium content.

Legumes and your diet

Some fad diets claim that compounds in raw legumes known as lectins cause inflammation. Lectins are anti-nutrients, meaning they can bind to minerals and prevent their absorption. Some theorize that lectins also bind to cells in the gut and lead to inflammation in the body. However, there is little research to back these claims.

Lectins are typically only an issue when consumed raw and can be removed through cooking. Since beans are enjoyed cooked and sometimes even soaked for long periods of time before cooking, lectins in beans are not a concern. For example, lectins in raw or improperly cooked kidney beans may cause severe stomach pain and food poisoning, but fully cooked kidney beans are safe to consume.

Legumes can be enjoyed on vegan, vegetarian, gluten-free, heart-healthy, and diabetes-friendly diets. Individuals with kidney disease who have been instructed to reduce potassium intake may need to limit beans. Finally, beans are typically not suitable for keto diets due to their carbohydrate content.

VARIETIES TO TRY

- *Black beans: Versatile, earthy, these make a delicious addition to tacos and salads*
- *Chickpeas: Eat them in soups or salads and blend into hummus*
- *Cannellini beans: Soft and creamy, these can be enjoyed blended or whole*
- *Lentils: These cook more quickly than other dried beans and offer an earthy, nutty flavor*
- *Green peas: Frozen peas can be added to dishes straight from the freezer*
- *Black-eyed peas: Serve with collard greens for a Southern-inspired dish and good luck on New Year's Day*
- *Kidney beans: Transform a can of these mild beans into a pot of chili*
- *Lima beans: Simmer with broth, herbs, onion, and garlic for a hearty side or main dish*
- *Peanuts: Yes, they are legumes, too! Enjoy peanut butter on apples for a crunchy snack*

DID YOU KNOW? *Beans are a great addition to baked goods! Substitute mashed or puréed beans for oil or butter in a 1:1 ratio in recipes for brownies and muffins.*

Opposite, top: Lentils bring earthy overtones to a filling salad lunch. Bottom: Chickpeas replace chicken and yogurt swaps in for mayo in this vegetarian, kale-based Caesar salad.

[SOY]

Soybeans pack a significant amount of fiber and protein and an array of micronutrients. They contain plant compounds that may help fight inflammation, including isoflavones, a type of phytoestrogen. Consumption of soy isoflavones has been associated with reduced blood levels of inflammation markers, such as CRP.

Choosing Soy

There are several soy-based foods and products available. Edamame are typically sold in the frozen food aisle or in containers in the produce section. Health food stores and larger grocery chains have a wider variety of soy foods, including a selection of dried and canned soybeans, soy milks and yogurts, tofu, tempeh, and miso.

In the Kitchen

Choose minimally processed soy products, such as soybeans and edamame, tofu, unsweetened soy milk and yogurt, and soy nuts. Less processed, whole soy foods provide more anti-inflammatory nutrients and compounds and are less likely to have added salt, sugar, or preservatives.

HOW TO EAT MORE

- *Snack on steamed edamame and sea salt*
- *Grill tofu brushed with olive oil, soy sauce, maple syrup, and garlic for a plant-based main dish*
- *Make overnight oats or chia pudding with unsweetened soy milk*

DID YOU KNOW?

Tempeh and miso are fermented soy foods and may offer additional benefits (see page 139).

NUTRITION PER
1 CUP COOKED EDAMAME

Calories	189
Fat	8 g
Protein	17 g
Carbohydrates	15 g
Fiber	8 g
Natural Sugars	3.4 g
Sodium	9 mg
Potassium	676 mg

SOY AND YOUR DIET

Soy foods are typically vegetarian and vegan, and many are gluten-free. Depending on their carbohydrate content, some soy foods may not fit into very low-carb or keto diets.

Consumption of minimally processed soy foods has been linked with a lower risk of inflammation-related diseases, including heart disease, stroke, type 2 diabetes, and certain cancers. Isoflavones in soy have weak estrogen-like effects in the body, leading some to believe that soy increases the risk of hormone-associated cancers, including breast, endometrial, and prostate cancer. However, most studies suggest that soy either has no impact on the development of these cancers or actually offers protection against them.

Soy may interfere with the absorption of thyroid hormone replacement medication. If you have a thyroid condition or take thyroid medication, speak with your doctor about eating soy.

[SALMON]

The anti-inflammatory properties of salmon are well-known, and for good reason! This fatty fish is a rich source of omega-3 fatty acids known as eicosapentaenoic acid (EPA) and docosahexaenoic acid (DHA). Omega-3s help calm inflammation, possibly by decreasing the production of inflammatory compounds and interfering with related processes in the body.

Choosing Salmon

Sockeye and king salmon tend to be higher in omega-3s than other varieties, but all kinds of salmon provide these fatty acids. If possible, choose wild-caught salmon over farmed. The omega-3 content of frozen salmon is similar to fresh.

In the Kitchen

Cooking techniques that remove moisture, such as smoking or curing, yield more omega-3s per serving. For the same reason, canned salmon also tends to have more omega-3s per serving than fresh. Just be mindful of the sodium content of these varieties, and choose reduced sodium or no-added-salt options, especially if you are watching your salt intake.

HOW TO EAT MORE

- *Enjoy poached or baked salmon with roasted vegetables for dinner (see page 150)*
- *Mix canned salmon with seasonings, ground oats, and eggs to make salmon "burgers"*

DID YOU KNOW?

Farmed salmon has a lot more omega-6 fatty acids, which can interfere with the anti-inflammatory effects of omega-3s when consumed in high doses.

NUTRITION PER
3 OZ COOKED SOCKEYE SALMON

Calories	143
Fat	6 g
Protein	22 g
Carbohydrates	0 g
Fiber	0 g
Natural Sugars	0 g
Sodium	114 mg
Potassium	347 mg

SALMON AND YOUR DIET

Salmon is a healthy addition to a wide range of special diets, including low-carb, keto, and gluten-free eating patterns. It contains no carbohydrates, while packing a significant amount of filling protein and fat, and therefore does not cause blood sugar spikes. Those with diabetes can pair foods that contain carbohydrates, such as fruit, starchy vegetables, and whole grains, with salmon to create a balanced meal.

Adding more salmon to your diet is a good choice for those aiming to prevent or manage heart disease. Eating two servings of fish that's high in omega-3 fatty acids per week can help reduce the risk of stroke and heart attack. These benefits may be even more apparent when fish replaces proteins that are high in saturated fat, such as processed meats and fatty cuts of red meat.

[OTHER FATTY FISH/SHELLFISH]

- A SPLASH OF HEALTHY OILS -

Salmon (see page 101) is one of the best-known sources of omega-3 fatty acids, but several other types of fish and shellfish offer these anti-inflammatory nutrients, too. Also known as oily fish, they include albacore tuna, herring, sardines, mackerel, trout, anchovies, mussels, and oysters.

Choosing Fatty Fish

To keep your fish at a safe temperature while grocery shopping, pick it up last, just before you get in the checkout line. Wrap it in a plastic bag to prevent cross-contamination with other foods. Seafood that has a pronounced fishy smell has gone bad and should be discarded.

In the Kitchen

Poaching, baking, and grilling do not have a significant impact on the anti-inflammatory potential of seafood. However, frying fish can take away some of its health benefits. Deep-frying can lead to the degradation of omega-3 fatty acids in addition to contributing unhealthy fats from frying oils.

HOW TO EAT MORE

• Make an open-face sandwich with rye bread, butter, pickled or smoked herring, and fresh dill

• Add anchovies to salads

• Enjoy mussels with broth, olive oil, garlic, and parsley over pasta

DID YOU KNOW?

Frozen fish is commonly mistaken for being nutritionally inferior to fresh fish. However, it is just as nutritious as fresh options and is usually less expensive.

NUTRITION PER
3 PACIFIC OYSTERS, COOKED

Calories	123
Fat	3.6 g
Protein	14.1 g
Carbohydrates	7.5 g
Fiber	0 g
Natural Sugars	0 g
Sodium	159 mg
Potassium	228 mg

FATTY FISH AND YOUR DIET

As long as you are not allergic to fish or shellfish, seafood can be enjoyed on heart-healthy, diabetes-friendly, low-carb, and gluten-free eating plans. The fish listed here are particularly good sources of anti-inflammatory omega-3s. Other types of fish and shellfish that are less oily, such as cod, shrimp, and scallops, are still very nutritious but have lower omega-3 contents.

Fish contains mercury, a toxic metal that may contribute to neurological issues and other health problems in high doses. Pregnant women, breastfeeding mothers, and young children should limit consumption of seafood with high levels of mercury, such as albacore tuna and swordfish. King mackerel tends to have more mercury than Atlantic mackerel.

[WALNUTS]

- THE ALA POWERHOUSES -

Highly concentrated in antioxidants and polyphenols that combat oxidative stress, walnuts have impressive anti-inflammatory properties. They contain ellagitannins that get converted by gut bacteria to urolithins, compounds that are being explored for their anti-cancer and inflammation-fighting effects. Walnuts are loaded with an omega-3 fatty acid known as alpha-linolenic acid (ALA) that may lower inflammation.

Choosing Walnuts

Walnuts are typically shelled before being sold. Inspect shelled walnuts for discoloration and mold, and avoid shriveled nuts. Keep walnuts in the refrigerator to extend their shelf life.

In the Kitchen

Both raw and roasted plain walnuts provide benefits. They do not have many nutritional differences, but raw nuts may have more antioxidants. If you prefer roasted walnuts, choose dry-roasted varieties that have been cooked with dry heat instead of oil.

HOW TO EAT MORE

• *Make a salad with walnuts, apples, red onion, lettuce, and balsamic dressing*

• *Add walnuts to breakfast yogurt or oatmeal*

• *Use chopped walnuts in place of half of the ground beef or turkey in taco meat*

DID YOU KNOW?

Roasting walnuts for short periods of time can bring out their flavor and reduce any bitter taste.

NUTRITION PER
1 OZ RAW, UNSALTED
WALNUTS (14 HALVES)

Calories	185
Fat	18 g
Protein	4.3 g
Carbohydrates	3.9 g
Fiber	1.9 g
Natural Sugars	0.7 g
Sodium	1 mg
Potassium	125 mg

WALNUTS AND YOUR DIET

On their own, walnuts are vegetarian, vegan, gluten-free, and low-carb. Due to their high fat content, they are a good addition to keto diets. People with allergies to tree nuts should avoid walnuts. In addition, raw nuts may exacerbate symptoms of IBD flare-ups.

The healthy fats, micronutrients, and plant compounds in walnuts may help reduce the risk of heart disease and stroke. If you have high blood pressure and are watching your sodium intake, purchase walnuts that do not have added salt.

Not all foods that contain walnuts are fitting for an anti-inflammatory diet— for example, baked goods made with sugar and butter and desserts made with candied walnuts. The best way to reap the anti-inflammatory potential of walnuts is to enjoy them plain or add your own healthy seasonings, such as olive oil, herbs, and spices.

[ALMONDS]

- VITAMIN E BOOSTERS -

Almonds are an excellent source of vitamin E, a fat-soluble nutrient that bestows antioxidant activity in the body. Regular consumption of almonds may also help reduce the risk of heart disease, in part due to the anti-inflammatory action of phytonutrients and heart-healthy monounsaturated fats they contain.

Choosing Almonds

Almonds are available raw, roasted, or blanched. Whole almonds typically have the best flavor. Underneath their brown skin, almonds should be uniformly white in color. Store almonds in an airtight container in a cool, dry, and dark place or in the refrigerator or freezer.

In the Kitchen

Similar to other nuts, raw and roasted plain almonds are comparable in nutrition. It's best to purchase roasted almonds that have been dry-roasted without the addition of unhealthy oils and without excess salt, sugar, or flavorings. Choose almond butters that have a single ingredient—almonds.

HOW TO EAT MORE

• *Make a trail mix with almonds, dried cherries, and shredded coconut*
• *Stir almond butter into breakfast oatmeal or add it to smoothies*
• *Sprinkle slivered almonds into salads*

DID YOU KNOW?

Almond milk is another way to enjoy these anti-inflammatory nuts. Look for unsweetened varieties without unnecessary additives.

NUTRITION PER
1 OZ RAW, UNSALTED ALMONDS (24 ALMONDS)

Calories	164
Fat	14.2 g
Protein	6 g
Carbohydrates	6.1 g
Fiber	3.5 g
Natural Sugars	1.2 g
Sodium	0 mg
Potassium	210 mg

ALMONDS AND YOUR DIET

Those who are not allergic to tree nuts can incorporate almonds into their meals. They are vegan, vegetarian, gluten-free, and low-carb. Their high fat content makes them a versatile ingredient for keto recipes. In fact, almond flour is commonly used in keto and gluten-free baked goods.

Eating almonds is beneficial for most inflammatory conditions, including heart disease, diabetes, arthritis, and psoriasis. However, those with IBD may have a difficult time digesting raw almonds and other raw nuts.

Raw almonds have been linked to salmonella outbreaks in the past. There have been no recent outbreaks, however, largely due to the implementation of a mandatory pasteurization program for almonds grown in California by the United States Department of Agriculture (USDA) in 2007.

[BRAZIL NUTS]

Brazil nuts are very rich in selenium, packing more than the daily recommended intake in just one nut. This essential mineral acts as an antioxidant in the body by protecting cells from oxidative damage, which contributes to inflammation and the development of related diseases. Getting enough selenium from your diet may also help decrease blood levels of CRP, a marker of inflammation.

NUTRITION PER
1 OZ RAW, UNSALTED BRAZIL NUTS (6 NUTS)

Calories	186
Fat	19 g
Protein	4.1 g
Carbohydrates	3.5 g
Fiber	2.1 g
Natural Sugars	0.7 g
Sodium	1 mg
Potassium	187 mg

Choosing Brazil Nuts

You can purchase Brazil nuts in raw, roasted, or blanched forms. Unless they have been blanched, Brazil nuts typically have spotty patches of brown skin on top of their white flesh. Avoid Brazil nuts that are shriveled or discolored.

In the Kitchen

The nutrition of Brazil nuts is similar across preparation methods. Since minerals are generally not heat-sensitive, roasted Brazil nuts maintain their selenium content. Be sure to purchase roasted Brazil nuts that have been cooked with dry heat, instead of with unhealthy oils.

BRAZIL NUTS AND YOUR DIET

The high-fat, low-carb content of Brazil nuts makes them suitable for keto diets. They are also naturally vegan, vegetarian, and gluten-free. However, individuals who are allergic to tree nuts need to avoid Brazil nuts. Like other raw nuts, raw Brazil nuts may be difficult to digest if you have IBD.

The majority of the fats in Brazil nuts are unsaturated and therefore beneficial for those who need to eat a heart-healthy diet. If you are watching your sodium intake, choose unsalted Brazil nuts.

Eating too many Brazil nuts may lead to excess intake of selenium. Over time, consuming very high amounts of selenium can cause brittle hair and nails, skin rashes, metallic taste, and even difficulty breathing and heart or kidney failure in severe cases. To avoid exceeding the daily upper limit for selenium, keep your intake of Brazil nuts at one to three per day.

HOW TO EAT MORE

• *Have one Brazil nut a day to meet your selenium needs*
• *Chop Brazil nuts and add to yogurt or oatmeal*
• *Have a couple Brazil nuts and a few slices of dried mango for a snack*

DID YOU KNOW?

Depending on your location, Brazil nuts may not be widely available. Try natural food stores and online retailers if you have trouble locating them.

[PECANS]

A wide variety of nutrients and compounds in pecans may contribute to their anti-inflammatory effects. In addition to providing monounsaturated fats and dietary fiber, pecans contain vitamin E and many polyphenols that act as antioxidants. Research shows that daily consumption of pecans may help lower low-density lipoprotein (LDL) and cholesterol levels and reduce heart disease risk.

NUTRITION PER
1 OZ RAW PECANS (19 HALVES)

Calories	196
Fat	20 g
Protein	2.6 g
Carbohydrates	3.9 g
Fiber	2.7 g
Natural Sugars	1.1 g
Sodium	0 mg
Potassium	116 mg

Choosing Pecans

Shelled pecan halves are commonly available. They should be plump and have a uniform brown color. Intact pecan halves tend to have a fresher taste than chopped pecans, but the latter is a good time-saving option. Store pecans in the refrigerator or freezer for best quality.

In the Kitchen

Raw and roasted plain pecans are both beneficial, as the nutrition of pecans is not significantly affected by roasting. As with other nuts, dry-roasted varieties are healthier than roasted pecans made with oils, salt, sugar, and/or flavorings.

HOW TO EAT MORE

• *Use chopped pecans, mixed with herbs and spices, as a coating for fish*

• *Add pecans to yogurt parfaits, breakfast oatmeal, or fruit salads*

• *Add pecans to baked goods*

DID YOU KNOW?

Pecans are native to North America, with up to 90% of the world's pecans grown in the US. The name comes from an Algonquin word describing nuts that had to be cracked open by stone.

PECANS AND YOUR DIET

Pecans are often candied or used in pies and other sweets. These preparations are not the healthiest way to eat more pecans for their anti-inflammatory benefits. Stick to eating raw or dry-roasted pecans and adding your own seasonings, especially if you need to watch your sugar or salt intake or have diabetes or heart disease.

Some people may be concerned with the high fat content of pecans and other nuts, especially if they have been told to reduce fat intake. However, pecans contain mostly monounsaturated and polyunsaturated fats, which are heart-healthy and provide many benefits when consumed in appropriate portions.

The fat content of pecans also makes them a good choice for those following a keto diet. Pecans are vegan, vegetarian, and gluten-free but should be avoided if you have a tree nut allergy. Raw nuts may worsen symptoms of flare-ups for those with IBD.

[CHIA SEEDS]

– BITE-SIZED HEALTHY FATS –

Though they are very small in size, chia seeds are an excellent source of dietary fiber, healthy fats, and nutrients that support anti-inflammatory processes. The fat in chia seeds mostly comes from the omega-3 fatty acid ALA, which may help reduce levels of inflammation markers. Chia seeds also offer antioxidant compounds, including kaempferol, quercetin, and caffeic acid.

Choosing Chia Seeds

Chia seeds have a very mild taste that's slightly nutty. They can be black or white in color, which have slight differences in their nutrition but are equally beneficial. Avoid brown chia seeds, since they are immature and not as nutritious.

In the Kitchen

Raw, soaked, and cooked chia seeds offer anti-inflammatory benefits. Chia seeds absorb water and form a gelatinous texture when combined with liquids. This contributes to their versatility.

HOW TO EAT MORE

- *Make chia seed pudding (see page 144)*
- *Use chia seeds in place of pectin to thicken jams and jellies*
- *Add chia seeds to smoothies, baked goods, homemade granolas, and salad dressings*

DID YOU KNOW?

Chia seeds come from a plant in the mint family that's native to Central America. They were a staple for the Aztecs and Mayans and are now widely available in the US.

NUTRITION PER
1 OZ (ABOUT 2 TBSP) CHIA SEEDS

Calories	138
Fat	9 g
Protein	4.7 g
Carbohydrates	12 g
Fiber	10 g
Natural Sugars	0 g
Sodium	5 mg
Potassium	115 mg

CHIA SEEDS AND YOUR DIET

The remarkable nutritional profile of chia seeds makes them a nutrient-dense choice for all types of diets. They do not contribute to blood sugar spikes, since they are very high in healthy fats and fiber and have no natural sugars. Thus, chia seeds may help those with diabetes maintain good blood sugar levels.

Chia seeds can help close nutritional and culinary gaps in plant-based diets. They are a complete protein source, meaning they have all of the essential amino acids that need to be obtained from foods. In addition, chia seeds can be mixed with water to replace eggs in vegan baking.

The high fiber content of chia seeds can lead to bloating, gas, constipation, or diarrhea. Incorporate chia seeds into your diet slowly and in moderate amounts for better tolerance. If you have IBD, digestive issues, or a condition that requires you to monitor fiber intake, you may want to limit your consumption of chia seeds.

[FLAXSEEDS]

The ALA fatty acids found in flaxseeds contribute to their inflammation-fighting potential. These seeds also contain lignans, which are polyphenols that have antioxidant, anti-inflammatory, and estrogen-like properties. Evidence suggests that flaxseed lignans may help reduce CRP levels and modulate inflammation in the intestines.

Choosing Flaxseeds

Choose ground flaxseeds over whole ones, since they are more easily digested and have more accessible nutrients and compounds. Flaxseed oil is also available and is more concentrated in ALA than flaxseeds but does not contain fiber. Flaxseeds and their oil have a subtle taste with nutty hints.

In the Kitchen

The ALA and lignans in ground flaxseeds appear to hold up under heat. Thus, ground flaxseeds can be eaten raw or added to baked goods and cooked dishes. However, flaxseed oil is sensitive to high heat, oxygen, and light. It is best used in cold meals, such as salads, or dishes that have already been cooked.

HOW TO EAT MORE

- Stir ground flaxseeds into oatmeal
- Add flaxseed meal to muffins and breads, or use it in pancake or waffle batters
- Use flaxseed oil as a salad dressing

NUTRITION PER
1 TBSP GROUND FLAXSEEDS

Calories	37
Fat	3 g
Protein	1.3 g
Carbohydrates	2 g
Fiber	1.9 g
Natural Sugars	0.1 g
Sodium	2 mg
Potassium	57 mg

FLAXSEEDS AND YOUR DIET

On their own, flaxseeds are vegetarian, vegan, gluten-free, and low-carb. Their fiber content can help blunt increases in blood sugar, making them a good food for individuals with diabetes. Flaxseeds can lead to constipation, diarrhea, and stomach upset in high doses. Remember to drink plenty of water when adding flaxseed to your diet.

People with psoriasis, eczema, lupus, arthritis, IBD, or other gastrointestinal conditions may have been advised to eat flaxseed to soothe inflammation. Currently, there is limited research on the use of flaxseed in the prevention and treatment of these conditions, but more studies are underway.

DID YOU KNOW?

Flaxseeds can be used in place of eggs in baking. Combine 1 tbsp of ground flaxseeds with 3 tbsp of water, stir, and let sit for 10 to 15 minutes to thicken.

[HEMP SEEDS]

- FATTY ACID HEROES -

Underneath the tough outer shell of hemp seeds lie nutrient-packed hemp hearts, which are rich in healthy fats, including both omega-3 and omega-6 essential fatty acids in a healthful ratio. Gamma-linolenic acid (GLA), an omega-6 in hemp seeds, has been shown to have potent anti-inflammatory properties in animal and test tube studies.

Choosing Hemp Seeds

Hemp hearts can either be white or light green. Their taste is very mild, with sweet and nutty undertones. You can find hemp hearts in the nut and seed aisle or bulk goods area of grocery stores.

In the Kitchen

Hemp hearts are usually eaten raw, which is the best way to enjoy them to preserve nutrients. The healthy fats in hemp hearts are sensitive to heat and may break down during high-heat cooking methods like frying, but they seem to hold up during baking. Hemp oil should not be used for cooking and instead be added to cold or already cooked dishes.

HOW TO EAT MORE

- *Sprinkle onto salads, toast, yogurt, or oatmeal*
- *Add to smoothies, pesto, hummus, sauces, muffins, or energy bites*
- *Use hemp oil as a salad dressing or drizzle onto pasta, roasted vegetables, or grain bowls*

DID YOU KNOW?

Derived from the hemp plant, CBD (cannabidiol) oil is gaining momentum as a possible treatment for pain and inflammation associated with arthritis and other conditions.

NUTRITION PER
3 TBSP HULLED HEMP SEEDS
(HEMP HEARTS)

Calories	166
Fat	14.6 g
Protein	9.5 g
Carbohydrates	2.6 g
Fiber	1.2 g
Natural Sugars	0.5 g
Sodium	1.5 mg
Potassium	360 mg

HEMP SEEDS AND YOUR DIET

Hemp seeds are a good source of healthy fats, fiber and plant-based protein. They are a complete protein source, making them a beneficial addition to vegan and vegetarian diets. A serving of hemp seeds (3 tbsp) has more protein than an egg.

Hemp seeds are naturally gluten-free but may be processed in facilities that deal with gluten-containing grains. If you have celiac disease or need to follow a gluten-free diet for other reasons, purchase certified gluten-free hemp seeds.

Hemp protein powder is another form of hemp seeds that's widely available. This can be used in smoothies, oatmeal, and baked goods. However, some hemp powders contain additives and sweeteners. To avoid unnecessary or unhealthy ingredients, look for brands that have hemp protein powder as the only ingredient.

[OLIVE OIL]

Olive oil has been associated with several health benefits, which are in part mediated by the anti-inflammatory compounds it contains. Among the abundance of antioxidants in olive oil is a compound known as oleocanthal that has anti-inflammatory mechanisms comparable to ibuprofen. The main unsaturated fatty acid in olive oil, oleic acid, may also reduce inflammation.

Choosing Olive Oil

Olive oil is sensitive to light, air, and excess heat. To ensure that you're getting high-quality olive oil that hasn't been overly exposed to these elements, choose extra-virgin olive oil. Avoid varieties labeled as "light," which indicates they may have been refined, and buy olive oil in dark glass or metal containers.

In the Kitchen

Claims that the fatty acids and antioxidants in olive oil are unstable when exposed to high heat have been refuted by research. The anti-inflammatory properties of olive oil hold up during roasting, sautéing, stir-frying, and most other common cooking methods.

HOW TO EAT MORE

• *Cook with extra-virgin olive oil*
• *Use as a base for dressings and marinades*
• *Replace melted butter or refined vegetable oils with olive oil in baking*

DID YOU KNOW?

Olive oils with a peppery bite and pungent taste contain the highest amounts of polyphenol antioxidants. They are typically made from olives that have been harvested early.

NUTRITION PER
1 TBSP OLIVE OIL

Calories	119
Fat	14 g
Protein	0 g
Carbohydrates	0 g
Fiber	0 g
Natural Sugars	0 g
Sodium	0 mg
Potassium	0 mg

OLIVE OIL AND YOUR DIET

Olive oil is an excellent food to add to your diet to help fight inflammation. The anti-inflammatory properties of olive oil are considered one of the reasons why the Mediterranean diet is associated with a reduced risk of heart disease, diabetes, cancer, and Alzheimer's disease. Consuming olive oil may also help with symptoms of arthritis, gout, and IBD.

Olive oil fits into vegan, vegetarian, gluten-free, and keto eating patterns. It contains no carbohydrates and does not raise blood sugar. Even though it's high in fat, moderate consumption of olive oil has not been shown to increase the probability of weight gain.

Some people drink olive oil to reap the benefits, but this practice can lead to overconsumption. It's best to add olive oil to recipes and use it in cooking. In fact, pairing olive oil with foods that contain fat-soluble nutrients can help boost nutrient absorption.

[GINGER]

– PAIN-RELIEVING ROOT –

For centuries, ginger has been hailed as a remedy for all sorts of ailments, and its anti-inflammatory effects are indeed powerful. It has been shown to help reduce joint pain and stiffness associated with arthritis, and relieve menstrual pain. It may also help protect against diseases associated with chronic inflammation, including Alzheimer's.

NUTRITION PER
1 TBSP FRESHLY CHOPPED GINGER

Calories	6
Fat	0 g
Protein	0 g
Carbohydrates	1.2 g
Fiber	0 g
Sugars	0 g
Sodium	0 mg
Potassium	24 mg

Choosing Ginger

When choosing fresh ginger root at the store, look for thin yet firm skin that doesn't have wrinkles. Wrinkly skin is a sign that the ginger is old. Dried ginger is available in the spice aisle.

In the Kitchen

The anti-inflammatory effects of ginger appear to be similar regardless as to whether the ginger is raw, cooked, or dried. Some claim that ginger becomes more potent when heated or dried, due to the conversion of the active compound gingerol into shogaols. Still, both fresh and dried ginger offer significant health benefits!

HOW TO EAT MORE

- *Add to stir-fries, salad dressings, marinades, soups, and curries*
- *Slip a slice into hot herbal tea*
- *Grate fresh ginger root for a mellower taste*

DID YOU KNOW?

Ginger keeps best in the refrigerator. Place intact pieces of ginger root, tightly wrapped in plastic wrap or stored in an airtight bag, in the crisper drawer.

GINGER AND YOUR DIET

A little bit of ginger goes a long way, and this flavorful spice provides a ton of health benefits for almost no calories. Since ginger is meant to be consumed in small amounts, it contributes minimal macronutrients, vitamins, or minerals. As such, it's a great addition to nearly any special diet, including low-carb, keto, gluten-free, vegan, or vegetarian diets.

Ginger is also an excellent seasoning for those following a low-sodium diet to manage high blood pressure or kidney disease. Since it has such a strong flavor, you can often cut back or omit salt in recipes that use it.

However, if you suffer from heartburn, ginger may not be the best option for you. Too much ginger can contribute to acid reflux and even lead to diarrhea or stomach upset. Start with small amounts of ginger and monitor your symptoms to ensure that you don't go overboard.

[TURMERIC]

- CURCUMIN BOOSTER -

The main active compound in turmeric that gives it a yellow-orange color—curcumin—is a potent anti-inflammatory agent and antioxidant. Curcumin may help reduce the risk of inflammation-related conditions, including heart disease, depression, Alzheimer's disease, and some cancers. It's also been shown to ease symptoms of arthritis and exercise-induced muscle soreness.

Choosing Turmeric

Fresh turmeric looks similar to fresh ginger root, but has orange flesh. It is often found next to ginger root in the produce section. It has a slightly bitter, peppery taste. You will find dried turmeric in the spice aisle.

In the Kitchen

Curcumin is poorly absorbed and gets quickly eliminated from the body when consumed on its own. Combining turmeric with black pepper can increase the bioavailability of curcumin by up to 2000%. Eating it with a source of fat can also boost absorption. Cooking turmeric may decrease its antioxidant capacity but does not eliminate it entirely.

HOW TO EAT MORE

- *Combine turmeric with black pepper and olive oil and use on roasted vegetables, rice, and salads*
- *Use turmeric to spice up curries or soups*
- *Make a turmeric "latte" with warm coconut milk, turmeric, ginger, cinnamon, and vanilla*

DID YOU KNOW?

Turmeric will stain kitchen equipment during cooking. Be sure to clean your equipment right after cooking to prevent stains from settling.

NUTRITION PER
1 TBSP GROUND TURMERIC

Calories	29
Fat	0.3 g
Protein	0.9 g
Carbohydrates	6 g
Fiber	2 g
Natural Sugars	0.3 g
Sodium	2.5 mg
Potassium	196 mg

TURMERIC AND YOUR DIET

Turmeric fits into any special diet, packs a ton of health benefits even in small amounts, and is naturally vegetarian, vegan, gluten-free, and low-sodium. When purchasing dried turmeric, check the ingredient list to make sure it does not contain any fillers or additives that do not fit into your diet. Some turmeric powders may contain trace amounts of gluten-containing flours or food dyes.

Studies have found that curcumin supplements may be as effective as some medications, including drugs used to manage heart disease, arthritis, and depression. While these results are promising, it's important to note that research is still limited and has mostly focused on supplements instead of dietary intake of turmeric. Always discuss with your health care provider before taking curcumin supplements or using turmeric in high doses, especially if you are on medications.

[GARLIC]

Garlic has long been touted as a medicinal food. It may not be the miracle worker it's often cracked up to be, but it has anti-inflammatory properties nevertheless. This pungent bulb provides sulfur-containing compounds that may suppress pro-inflammatory cytokines, including tumor necrosis factor-alpha (TNF-alpha) and interleukin-6 (IL-6).

Choosing Garlic

You can find garlic fresh, frozen, jarred, and dried. Fresh bulbs should have dry skin and firm, tightly packed cloves. Avoid any that have soft spots or mold. Keep in a cool, dark place in your kitchen. Dried garlic powder or minced garlic is kept in the spice aisle, and many stores carry garlic paste in the freezer aisle.

In the Kitchen

Crushing or chopping garlic releases an enzyme that leads to the formation of beneficial sulfurous compounds. To amplify the benefits, let crushed garlic sit for 10 to 15 minutes before using. Garlic that has been lightly cooked appears to have benefits comparable to raw cloves.

HOW TO EAT MORE

- *Use raw garlic in dressings and marinades*
- *Roast whole heads of garlic and squeeze out the cloves to use in spreads and soups*
- *Sauté vegetables in garlic and olive oil*

DID YOU KNOW?

Garlic cloves sprout over time. Sprouted garlic tends to have more antioxidants than younger garlic. The sprouts are safe to eat but often taste very bitter.

NUTRITION PER
1 CLOVE RAW GARLIC

Calories	4.5
Fat	0 g
Protein	0.2 g
Carbohydrates	1 g
Fiber	0.06 g
Natural Sugars	0.03 g
Sodium	0.5 mg
Potassium	12 mg

GARLIC AND YOUR DIET

Garlic packs a ton of flavor without a lot of extra calories, carbohydrates, or fat. It can be enjoyed on all types of special diets. If you are watching your sodium intake, garlic is an excellent substitution for salt and imparts a pungent flavor to dishes while contributing negligible amounts of sodium.

While garlic is generally safe for most people, it can have some unwanted side effects. Garlic, especially raw garlic, may lead to heartburn, nausea, burning in the mouth or stomach, or diarrhea. Eating a lot of garlic can also contribute to bad breath. To help neutralize garlic breath, consume apples or lemon juice alongside dishes with garlic.

Those on blood-thinning medications should avoid over-consuming garlic or taking garlic supplements, since they may increase the risk of bleeding. Consult with your health care provider before trying garlic supplements.

[CINNAMON]

– OXIDATIVE STRESS RELIEVER –

Cinnamon is very rich in antioxidants, providing your body with tools to ward off oxidative stress and resulting inflammation. Eating more cinnamon may also help in the management of inflammation-related diseases. Studies suggest that cinnamon can help lower blood sugar and cholesterol levels in those with diabetes.

Choosing Cinnamon

Cinnamon is most commonly enjoyed dried in powder form. Cinnamon sticks are also available and can be used in recipes that require simmering to impart delicious flavor. Since cinnamon has both sweet and spicy hints, it can be incorporated into a variety of dishes ranging from desserts to savory soups.

In the Kitchen

Cinnamon loses some of its antioxidant capacity during cooking. Keeping cinnamon raw and adding it to dishes after cooking may help preserve its healthy properties, but don't stress about doing this if it alters the flavor of your dish. Cooked cinnamon still provides benefits.

HOW TO EAT MORE

- *Sprinkle cinnamon onto yogurt, cereal, and fruit salads*
- *When preparing dried beans or lentils, add a cinnamon stick to the pot for extra flavor*
- *Replace sugar with cinnamon in your coffee*

DID YOU KNOW?

Ceylon cinnamon, native to Sri Lanka, is praised for its sweet and mild taste. It's not as widely available as cassia cinnamon, which has a stronger, more bitter flavor.

NUTRITION PER
1 TBSP GROUND CINNAMON

Calories	19
Fat	0.1 g
Protein	0.3 g
Carbohydrates	6 g
Fiber	4 g
Natural Sugars	0.2 g
Sodium	1 mg
Potassium	34 mg

CINNAMON AND YOUR DIET

Cinnamon is naturally vegetarian, vegan, gluten-free, low-carb, and low-sodium. Individuals with diabetes may especially benefit from incorporating cinnamon into their meals due to its blood sugar-lowering effects. The spice is also being studied for its anti-cancer properties and potential for boosting brain health and preventing Alzheimer's disease.

Eating cinnamon in the amounts typically used in cooking is unlikely to be harmful. However, there may be some risks associated with consuming large amounts or taking cinnamon supplements. Cinnamon contains a compound known as coumarin that can cause liver toxicity in high doses and may interact with blood thinners. In addition, individuals on medications for diabetes should be cautious about consuming too much cinnamon to prevent blood sugar from falling too low.

[PARSLEY]

– RICH IN VITAMIN C –

Parsley is a source of carotenoid antioxidants and vitamin C. It also contains many beneficial compounds, including the flavonoid apigenin that has been shown to inhibit the expression of inflammatory markers.

Choosing Parsley

Fresh parsley exists in two forms: flat-leaf "Italian" and curly-leaf. Flat-leaf parsley tends to be more flavorful. Look for leaves that are bright green and blemish-free and have no signs of spoiling. To prolong its freshness, fresh parsley should be stored upright in a jar filled with a couple of inches of water in the refrigerator. If you can't find fresh parsley, check the spice aisle for dried versions.

In the Kitchen

Heating fresh parsley can degrade some of the vitamin C content, but drying herbs preserves antioxidants. In fact, dried parsley may contain up to 17 times more antioxidants than fresh parsley.

HOW TO EAT MORE

- *Add parsley to tomato sauce, soups, or salads*
- *Use fresh parsley in marinades, dressings, and dips, such as chimichurri sauce and pesto*
- *Make a parsley sauce to serve with fish (see page 150)*

NUTRITION PER
1 TBSP FRESHLY CHOPPED PARSLEY

Calories	2
Fat	0 g
Protein	0.2 g
Carbohydrates	0.4 g
Fiber	0.2 g
Natural Sugars	0 g
Sodium	4 mg
Potassium	42 mg

PARSLEY AND YOUR DIET

It is easy to add parsley to meals and it can be enjoyed on gluten-free, vegetarian, vegan, low-carb, and keto diets. By using parsley to flavor dishes in addition to, or in place of, salt, you can cut back on sodium intake.

However, parsley is high in vitamin K, a nutrient involved in blood clotting (see page 35). If you are taking blood-thinning medications, you are likely advised to keep vitamin K intake consistent. Keep that in mind if you plan to incorporate more parsley into your meals, and discuss with your health care provider or consult a dietitian before increasing your intake of parsley.

DID YOU KNOW?

Dried herbs can be substituted for fresh in a 1:3 ratio. For instance, use 1 teaspoon dried parsley in place of 3 teaspoons fresh.

[GREEN TEA]

Green tea is rich in epigallocatechin-3-gallate (EGCG), a polyphenol that can suppress inflammation processes in the body and acts as an antioxidant. EGCG has been shown to improve symptoms of IBD and arthritis and may protect against heart disease and cancer, and other conditions driven by inflammation.

Choosing Green Tea

You can purchase loose leaf green tea or tea bags. If you opt for loose leaves, use a tea infuser to steep about one teaspoonful per cup of hot water. There are also many iced green teas available, but they often contain added sugars or preservatives. Check the label to choose an unsweetened variety. Matcha, a type of powdered green tea, typically has more antioxidants than other green tea varieties due to how it's harvested.

In the Kitchen

Loose leaf green teas tend to have the highest EGCG contents. In addition, green teas labeled as first or shincha harvest are considered the highest quality.

HOW TO EAT MORE

- *Warm up with a cup of green tea*
- *Make iced green tea, and add lemon and mint for more flavor*
- *Use matcha powder in lattes and smoothies*

DID YOU KNOW?

Black tea and green tea come from the same plant and both have anti-inflammatory properties. However, green tea is higher in antioxidants.

NUTRITION PER
1 CUP BREWED GREEN TEA

Calories	2.5
Fat	0 g
Protein	0.5 g
Carbohydrates	0 g
Fiber	0 g
Natural Sugars	0 g
Sodium	2.5 mg
Potassium	20 mg

GREEN TEA AND YOUR DIET

Green tea contributes almost no calories and nutrients, while still being loaded with beneficial compounds, and is vegan, vegetarian, gluten-free, and low-carb. It can easily fit into several types of eating patterns. However, it's important to drink green tea in moderation.

Some green teas, especially bottled iced green tea, may contain added sugars or other ingredients that change its nutritional profile. If you are watching your sugar intake or have diabetes, check food labels and opt for unsweetened green teas. Green tea also contains caffeine and is therefore not a suitable choice for those who avoid or limit caffeine. Due to the presence of compounds that bind to minerals in green tea, drinking a lot of this beverage may reduce iron absorption. If you have low iron levels, drink green tea in between meals instead of with food.

[DARK CHOCOLATE]

- FULL OF FLAVONOLS -

Cocoa contains flavanols, which have powerful anti-inflammatory and antioxidant properties. The ORAC (oxygen radical absorption capacity) values of dark chocolate are comparable to those of berries. Dark chocolate may also protect against risk factors for heart disease, insulin resistance, and artery damage associated with aging.

Choosing Dark Chocolate

Choose dark chocolate with 70–85% cocoa and a low sugar content. The higher the percentage, the more antioxidants chocolate contains. However, it can have a bitter taste. To cut the bitterness, look for options combined with dried fruit or nuts or small amounts of natural sweeteners, such as honey or maple syrup.

In the Kitchen

Dark chocolate is often used in recipes with added sugar or high-fat ingredients. To avoid compromising the nutrition of dark chocolate, eat it on its own, or mix it with other nutritious ingredients and add it to lighter versions of baked goods.

HOW TO EAT MORE

- *Make chocolate bark: melt dark chocolate, spread it on a baking sheet lined with wax paper, and top with dried fruit and nuts. Refrigerate until chilled, and break into pieces.*
- *Add dark chocolate shavings to fruit salads, smoothies, or oatmeal.*

DID YOU KNOW?

Milk and white chocolate do not have as much cocoa as dark chocolate and so contain fewer beneficial compounds. They also contain higher amounts of added sugar and fat.

NUTRITION PER
1 OZ 70–85% DARK CHOCOLATE

Calories	170
Fat	12 g
Protein	2 g
Carbohydrates	13 g
Fiber	3 g
Natural Sugars	7 g
Sodium	5 mg
Potassium	203 mg

DARK CHOCOLATE AND YOUR DIET

If you follow a special diet, it's important to check the ingredients list on dark chocolate. Some varieties are vegan, while others are made with milk fat. Dark chocolate is naturally gluten-free but sometimes has gluten-containing ingredients added to it. Depending on the added sugar content, it may not suit low-carb or keto eating patterns. Furthermore, many manufacturers add soy lecithin to dark chocolate to bind the ingredients. This additive should be avoided by those with soy allergies.

Consuming dark chocolate in small amounts typically does not present concerns, but excess consumption could have side effects. Dark chocolate contains caffeine, so those who are sensitive to caffeine may want to limit consumption. Cocoa is also a source of oxalates, which can contribute to the formation of kidney stones. Keep this in mind if you have been advised to follow a low-oxalate diet to prevent stones.

[HONEY]

This natural, sweet syrup contains antioxidants that help balance out free radicals in the body that contribute to inflammation-driven diseases. It's considered a cough suppressant when consumed orally and may even soothe symptoms of inflammatory skin conditions, such as psoriasis, when applied topically.

Choosing Honey

Look for honey labeled as raw or pure, which means it hasn't been treated with heat or processing techniques that destroy antioxidants and trace minerals. Darker honeys tend to have more antioxidants than light-colored varieties. Due to its antimicrobial properties, honey has a long shelf life, and can usually last up to two years.

In the Kitchen

Honey has the highest antioxidant and antibacterial capacity when consumed raw, since heating causes beneficial compounds to break down. It can be used in cooked dishes and baked goods but won't have as many benefits.

HOW TO EAT MORE

- Drizzle honey on top of apple slices spread with peanut butter
- Use honey in place of sugar in healthy treats, such as energy bars (see page 156)
- Mix honey into marinades and dressings

DID YOU KNOW?

Manuka honey, from New Zealand, has strong anti-inflammatory effects and may be useful for promoting wound healing and soothing sore throats.

NUTRITION PER
1 TBSP HONEY

Calories	54
Fat	0 g
Protein	0.1 g
Carbohydrates	17 g
Fiber	0 g
Natural Sugars	17 g
Sodium	1 mg
Potassium	11 mg

HONEY AND YOUR DIET

Honey is a source of sugar and should be consumed in moderation. Use it in place of refined sugar or sweeteners for some bonus benefits, but don't go overboard.

Individuals with diabetes and those who follow a low-carb diet should view honey as a sweetener that contributes to the carb content of dishes. Honey raises blood sugar, but it may do so to a lesser extent than refined sugars.

If you have an inflammatory skin condition and are interested in trying honey as a topical treatment, discuss with a dermatologist first.

Some small studies and many anecdotal accounts support the theory that eating raw, local honey can help relieve seasonal allergies by decreasing sensitivity to local pollen. If you are interested in trying local honey to help with your seasonal allergies, use it in place of other sweeteners in your diet.

[YOGURT]

It's believed that the anti-inflammatory properties in yogurt stem from probiotics— "good" bacteria used in the fermentation process. Probiotics support a healthy gut microbiome, a strong intestinal lining, and optimal immunity. Consuming foods with probiotics may reduce blood levels of inflammatory markers.

Choosing Yogurt

Look for brands that are unsweetened or contain minimal amounts of added sugars and other ingredients. Greek and Skyr yogurts are richer in protein and have thicker textures than other types. Some snacks may be coated in yogurt and therefore labeled as "healthy." However, yogurt coatings typically have small amounts of actual yogurt and are mostly made of sugar, oils, and additives.

In the Kitchen

Choose yogurt that has live and active cultures. Some of the common probiotics added on top of the initial cultures include *Lactobacillus acidophilus* and *Lactobacillus casei*. The former, in particular, has been associated with many health benefits.

HOW TO EAT MORE

- *Enjoy plain yogurt for breakfast, topped with fresh berries, almonds, and hemp seeds*
- *Make frozen yogurt bark by spreading yogurt on a lined baking sheet, adding desired toppings, and freezing for a couple of hours*

DID YOU KNOW?

While most studies support the anti-inflammatory effects of yogurt, more research is needed on other dairy products.

NUTRITION PER
7 OZ PLAIN, LOW-FAT GREEK YOGURT

Calories	146
Fat	3.8 g
Protein	20 g
Carbohydrates	7.9 g
Fiber	0 g
Natural Sugars	7 g
Sodium	68 mg
Potassium	282 mg

YOGURT AND YOUR DIET

People who have a dairy allergy or are lactose intolerant should not consume yogurt. Non-dairy yogurt that has active cultures, such as cultured coconut milk yogurt, and fermented foods (see page 139) are alternative sources of probiotics.

Yogurt can be added to vegetarian diets that include dairy products. It is also gluten-free, unless the ingredients list shows otherwise. Some yogurts, such as unsweetened Greek yogurt, may fit into a low-carb diet. Yogurt contains some natural sugars in the form of lactose, but is considered a low-GI food and does not drastically raise blood sugar.

Yogurt may not bring anti-inflammatory benefits to individuals who have high levels of inflammation in their body. In these instances, your health care provider may recommend eliminating dairy products for a period of time and then reintroducing them slowly so that you can assess your individual reaction.

[FERMENTED FOODS]

- GOOD BACTERIA -

Fermented foods are produced through the activity of yeast or bacteria that break down carbohydrates into alcohol, acids, or other nutrients. They are a source of probiotics in the diet, and eating them can increase the number and variety of healthy flora in your gut. By enhancing gut health, fermented foods support your body's anti-inflammatory processes.

Choosing Fermented Foods

In addition to yogurt and kefir, fermented foods include sauerkraut, kimchi, miso paste (fermented soybeans and grains), tempeh (fermented soybeans formed into a block), and kombucha. Pickles and other pickled vegetables may also be fermented foods, but only if their labels indicate that they have been "lacto-fermented." Always choose options that have minimal ingredients. Some varieties of kombucha may have added sugars, so be sure to check the label.

In the Kitchen

Many probiotic cultures are sensitive to heat. Thus, it's best to add fermented foods to meals towards the end of cooking to maintain their healthy bacteria.

HOW TO EAT MORE

• *Make a salad dressing with olive oil, miso paste, lemon juice, and ginger*
• *Add kimchi or sauerkraut to grain bowls*
• *Sip on kombucha for an afternoon pick-me-up*

DID YOU KNOW?

Tempeh is a complete protein source and contains all of the essential amino acids. This makes it a good choice for vegans and vegetarians.

NUTRITION PER
1 TBSP WHITE MISO PASTE

Calories	35
Fat	1 g
Protein	2 g
Carbohydrates	4 g
Fiber	1 g
Natural Sugars	1 g
Sodium	740 mg
Potassium	34 mg

FERMENTED FOODS AND YOUR DIET

Fermented foods may lead to unpleasant digestive symptoms in high doses. Some people experience bloating, gas, and stomach discomfort after consuming these foods, especially if they are trying them for the first time.

Certain fermented foods are high in salt. They include miso paste, sauerkraut, and kimchi. They may need to be limited if you have high blood pressure or have been advised to decrease sodium intake for medical reasons. Fermented foods may not fit other diets depending on their ingredients and nutritional profile. Miso paste and tempeh can have gluten-containing ingredients, for example.

Fermented foods are high in histamines, compounds involved in allergic and immune responses. Individuals with histamine intolerance cannot break down dietary histamine and may want to limit fermented foods.

RECIPES

So, you've stocked your kitchen with anti-inflammatory foods … now what? This section will help you put your newfound knowledge about anti-inflammatory eating into practice! Here are eight delicious recipes to get you started: two each for breakfast, lunch, dinner, and snacks. You'll recognize many of the foods on the ingredient lists, including fruits, vegetables, salmon, olive oil, herbs and other flavor boosters, yogurt, and more.

Healthy eating may seem intimidating and time-consuming, but it truly can be convenient and affordable with the right recipes and mindset. These no-fuss recipes are intended to showcase just that. They all have short prep times and ingredient lists, and many can be prepared in advance for easy eating during busy weeks. Plus, there are tons of tips for how to customize the dishes to meet your or your family's dietary needs.

DID YOU KNOW?

Experts believe that combinations of nutrients and compounds in whole foods work together to provide the greatest anti-inflammatory effects. To benefit most, eat whole foods instead of taking supplements with specific nutrients.

BERRY KIWI YOGURT PARFAITS

–
YOGURT PAGE 137
BERRIES PAGES 67, 68
KIWI PAGE 85
POMEGRANATE PAGE 81
OATS PAGE 89
–

- MAKES 4 SERVINGS -

Start your morning with an easy, prep-ahead dish that's full of anti-inflammatory goodness. The Greek yogurt provides satiating protein to keep you full all morning, while its probiotic content supports a healthy gut. Berries and pomegranates are both antioxidant powerhouses and the kiwi contributes a zingy burst of vitamin C. Together these fruits add plenty of natural sweetness, eliminating the need for a sugary yogurt. In between these layers, the oats add fiber, more antioxidants, and the essential mineral selenium.

Method

1. Gather four glass jars or airtight containers with lids.

2. Prepare the parfaits by adding a layer of yogurt to the bottom of each jar, followed by a few berries, kiwi slices, pomegranate arils, and a sprinkle of granola.

3. Continue alternating layers of yogurt and toppings, and drizzle with a small amount of honey, if desired.

4. Enjoy immediately, or seal the containers and store in the refrigerator for up to a few days.

INGREDIENTS

1 quart Greek yogurt
2 cups berries of choice (strawberries, blueberries, loganberries, blackberries)
2 kiwis, peeled and sliced
1/2 cup pomegranate arils
1 cup oat-based granola
Honey, to taste (optional)

EASY ALTERNATIVES

- *For a dairy-free version, opt for cultured coconut milk yogurt.*

- *If you prefer different fruits, choose from the other anti-inflammatory options in this book—grapes, pineapple, cherries, or oranges—for example.*

GRANOLA TIPS

Use homemade or store-bought
granola with nuts, unsweetened
dried fruits, and minimal amounts
of added sugars and unhealthy oils.
No granola? Use sliced almonds or
chopped walnuts or pecans instead.

CHERRY CHIA PUDDING

–
CHIA SEEDS PAGE 113
ALMONDS (MILK) PAGE 107
CHERRIES PAGE 71
–

– MAKES 4 SERVINGS –

When combined with liquid, chia seeds develop a gelatinous texture that's ideal for a healthy pudding. This high-fiber breakfast promotes gut health and its anti-inflammatory benefits are wide-reaching. ALA omega-3 fatty acids in the seeds support anti-inflammatory processes and both the chia seeds and the cherries contain antioxidants. Bringing the flavor up a notch and providing juicy, sweet notes in every bite, the cherries also contain anthocyanin pigments, which can help with exercise recovery.

INGREDIENTS

½ cup chia seeds
2 cups unsweetened almond milk or milk of choice
1 tsp vanilla extract
2 tsp honey or maple syrup (optional)
3 cups pitted cherries, fresh or frozen
Plain yogurt, for layering (optional)

Method

1. Gather four glass jars or airtight containers with lids.

2. In a large bowl, whisk together the chia seeds, almond milk, vanilla, and honey or maple syrup, if using. Divide the chia mixture evenly among the containers and seal them. Transfer to the refrigerator and let the pudding sit for at least a few hours, and preferably overnight, to thicken.

3. Add 2 cups of cherries and 4 tablespoons of water to a saucepan. Cook over medium-low heat for about 15 minutes, stirring frequently and using the back of a fork to break down the cherries. When the mixture has thickened, cool, then store in an airtight container in the refrigerator.

4. Once the chia pudding has set, open the jars and add a layer of cherry compote on top. Feel free to layer in some plain yogurt, if desired. Top with the remaining cherries, and enjoy!

EASY ALTERNATIVES

• *While the ingredients call for unsweetened almond milk, you can substitute other plant-based milks, including coconut milk, hemp milk, or oat milk.*

• *If you're a chocolate lover, add ¼ cup cacao powder or unsweetened cocoa powder to the chia seed mix.*

LUNCHTIME TIP

To boost the nutrition of your chia puddings even more, add sliced nuts or a spoonful of nut butter. Be sure to wash it down with water to help the fiber move through your body.

CARROT AND LENTIL SOUP

- MAKES 4 SERVINGS -

Carrots are rich in beta-carotene, which serves as an antioxidant, while lentils provide plenty of polyphenols and inflammation-fighting compounds. Curry powder gets its orange color from curcumin-loaded turmeric. The garlic and red pepper flakes contribute sulfur- and capsaicin-containing compounds.

Method

1. Heat the olive oil in a large soup pot over medium heat. Add the diced onion and cook for 5 minutes or until translucent. Stir in the garlic, ginger, curry powder, and red pepper flakes, and cook for a minute more until fragrant.

2. Add the sliced carrots, dried lentils, and vegetable stock to the pot. Increase the heat and bring to a boil, then reduce the heat to medium-low, cover, and cook for 30 to 35 minutes until the lentils are tender.

3. Uncover and turn off the heat. Use an immersion or hand blender to purée the soup in the pot. If you are using an upright blender instead, carefully transfer the soup to the blender. You may need to blend the soup in batches depending on your blender size.

4. Taste the soup, and add salt and pepper as needed. Serve hot, topped with chopped cilantro, a dollop of Greek yogurt, and an extra sprinkling of red pepper flakes, if desired.

–
GARLIC PAGE 125
GINGER PAGE 121
TURMERIC PAGE 123
CARROTS PAGE 43
LENTILS PAGES 95, 96
–

INGREDIENTS

2 tbsp extra-virgin olive oil
1 yellow onion, diced
5 cloves garlic, minced
1 tbsp freshly chopped ginger
1 tsp curry powder
1/4 tsp red pepper flakes
5 small carrots, sliced
3/4 cup dried red lentils
4 cups vegetable broth
Salt and pepper, to taste
Chopped cilantro, for topping
Greek yogurt, for topping

EASY ALTERNATIVES

- *Skip the yogurt to keep it vegan.*
- *Substitute white beans if you don't have lentils on hand.*

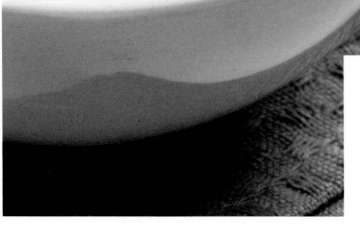

FREEZE IT!

Make this soup in advance for easy
lunches or dinners on busy days. To
freeze, transfer the soup to airtight
containers with lids, leaving an inch
of headspace to allow the soup to
expand while freezing. It will keep in
the freezer for up to six months.

LEMON CHICKPEA QUINOA SALAD

– MAKES 4 SERVINGS –

Packed with plant protein and flavor, this easy quinoa salad is a great lunch option that you can bring to work or eat at home. Quinoa is a source of prebiotic fiber that feeds healthy gut bacteria and provides an abundance of antioxidants. Here it is speckled with pomegranate arils, which count anti-aging effects among their many benefits. The ingredients are tossed in a lemon-olive oil dressing. The olive oil contributes healthy fats and helps with nutrient absorption, while the lemon brings a zesty burst of vitamin C.

INGREDIENTS

3 cups cooked quinoa
1 (15-oz) can chickpeas, drained
  and rinsed
1 cup pomegranate arils
¼ cup fresh mint leaves
½ chile pepper, seeded and finely
  sliced (optional)
3 tbsp extra-virgin olive oil
Zest of 1 lemon (optional)
1 lemon, juiced
¼ tsp salt
¼ tsp freshly ground pepper

Method

1. Combine the cooked quinoa, chickpeas, pomegranate arils, mint leaves, and chile pepper (if using) in a large mixing bowl.

2. In a separate bowl, whisk together the olive oil, lemon zest (if using), lemon juice, salt, and pepper.

3. Toss the salad with the dressing until well coated, and serve.

EASY ALTERNATIVES

- Increase the quantities to serve this dish as a main course with a side of roasted green beans and asparagus.

- For more protein, add sliced almonds, tofu, tempeh, shrimp, or salmon.

- For more antioxidants, choose tri-color, red, black, or yellow quinoa.

- For a different flavor, use lime juice and zest in place of lemon.

- Fresh mint can be swapped with parsley.

DOUBLE UP

You can always cook the quinoa a day or so in advance to cut back on prep time. Why not make a bulk quantity and use the leftovers in another dish later in the week?

SALMON WITH PARSLEY SAUCE

- MAKES 4 SERVINGS -

SALMON PAGE 101
SPINACH PAGE 35
YOGURT PAGE 137
PARSLEY PAGE 129

Served over a bed of wilted spinach and topped with a yogurt-based parsley sauce, this salmon dinner will delight both your taste buds and your health. Salmon is loaded with omega-3s that fight inflammation in the body, spinach provides provitamin A carotenoids and lutein, and parsley packs flavonoids that dampen inflammation.

Method

1. Preheat the oven to 425°F and line a baking sheet with foil.

2. Place the salmon fillets skin-side down on the baking sheet. Drizzle each fillet with olive oil, using your fingers to rub it into the flesh. Season with salt and pepper. Bake the salmon until it flakes with a fork and the internal temperature has reached 145°F, about 12 to 18 minutes depending on the thickness of the fillets.

3. Put the spinach in a large saucepan with an inch of water. Bring to a boil, cover, and cook for 2 to 3 minutes until wilted. Drain and set aside. If you have a steamer basket, use that for the spinach instead to preserve some of the nutrients.

4. In a mixing bowl, combine the yogurt, grated cucumber, minced garlic, parsley, lemon juice, and salt. Stir together.

5. Divide the wilted spinach evenly among four plates. Top each pile of spinach with a salmon fillet, followed by a dollop of parsley yogurt sauce. Sprinkle with more chopped parsley, if desired.

INGREDIENTS

4 salmon fillets, skin on
1 tbsp olive oil
Salt and pepper, to taste
8 cups baby spinach
2 cups Greek yogurt
1 cup grated cucumber
2 cloves garlic, minced
2 tbsp chopped fresh parsley
Juice of 1/2 lemon
1/4 tsp salt

EASY ALTERNATIVES

• *Replace the spinach with another leafy green, such as collard or mustard greens.*

MEASURE UP!

Want perfectly roasted salmon?
Take measure of the thickness of
your salmon fillets. Every half-inch
of thickness equates to 4 to 6 minutes
cooking time.

HOMEMADE BURRITO BOWLS

- MAKES 4 SERVINGS -

Enjoy all the usual burrito fix-ins in bowl form. This prep-friendly recipe combines an assortment of anti-inflammatory foods into a colorful and satisfying dinner. The rice and beans both contribute gut-nourishing fiber and an array of antioxidants to shield cells from damage. Sulfur-containing compounds give radishes their spicy kick, and broccoli is a source of the powerful antioxidant kaempferol. The olive oil, lime, and honey dressing combines three anti-inflammatory stalwarts.

Method

1. To steam the broccoli, bring a couple inches of water to a boil in a large pot. Place a steamer basket into the pot, add the broccoli florets, cover, and cook for 5 to 7 minutes until crisp-tender. If you don't have a steamer basket, add the broccoli to an inch of boiling water in a large skillet, cover, and cook for a few minutes before draining.

2. Divide the rice, black beans, broccoli, tomatoes, spinach, avocado, and radishes evenly among four bowls.

3. In a small bowl, whisk together the olive oil, lime juice, cilantro, honey, and salt. Pour the dressing over the burrito bowls, and enjoy.

BROCCOLI PAGES 37, 39
RICE PAGE 93
BLACK BEANS PAGES 95, 96
TOMATOES PAGE 63
SPINACH PAGE 35
AVOCADOS PAGE 65
RADISHES PAGES 37, 38

INGREDIENTS

2 cups broccoli florets
2 cups cooked rice of your choice
2 (15-oz) cans black beans, drained and rinsed
2 cups halved cherry tomatoes
2 cups baby spinach
2 avocados, sliced
4 radishes, sliced
1/2 cup extra-virgin olive oil
Juice of 2 limes
1/4 cup chopped fresh cilantro
2 tsp honey
1/4 tsp salt

EASY ALTERNATIVES

- *Substitute wild for brown rice for a stronger, nuttier taste.*

- *In place of tomatoes and avocados, add salsa and guacamole (see page 154) for some extra spice and flavor.*

CUSTOMIZE IT

Burrito bowls are also fit for the entire family, since each person can build their own depending on personal tastes and dietary needs.

SPICY GUACAMOLE WITH FRESH VEGGIES

AVOCADOS PAGE 65
TOMATOES PAGE 63
PEPPERS PAGE 61
CITRUS PAGE 79

- MAKES 4 SERVINGS -

An ideal condiment or snack, homemade guacamole is a powerhouse of compounds that help attack inflammation. The monounsaturated fats in avocados promote heart health, while fiber boosts digestion and the vegetables used for serving contain an assortment of essential nutrients. Jalapeño and chile peppers get their heat from anti-inflammatory capsaicin and tomatoes contribute lycopene, which helps mitigate inflammatory processes in the body.

INGREDIENTS

4 ripe avocados
1/2 cup chopped tomatoes
1/2 cup chopped red onion
1 jalapeño, seeded and finely sliced
1 chile pepper, seeded and finely sliced
2 garlic cloves, minced
1/4 cup chopped fresh cilantro
Juice of 1 lime
Salt, to taste
Vegetables for serving: carrots, cauliflower, celery, bell peppers, radishes, roasted sweet potatoes

Method

1. Slice the avocados in half lengthwise and carefully remove their pits. Cut the flesh into cubes and scoop into a large mixing bowl.

2. Add the chopped tomatoes, red onion, jalapeño, chile pepper, garlic, and cilantro. Gently stir to combine all the ingredients.

3. Squeeze the lime juice over the avocado mixture, and sprinkle with salt to taste. Taste, and adjust seasonings as desired.

4. Serve the guacamole with fresh vegetables of your choice.

EASY ALTERNATIVES

- *If you shy away from heat, skip the jalapeño and chile peppers and use a bell pepper instead.*
- *Guacamole also tastes delicious with such additions as sweet corn, pineapple, pomegranate arils, and apples.*
- *Serve guacamole with burrito bowls (see page 152), tacos, salads, beans, or rice, as a nourishing side.*

KEEP IT FRESH

To avoid the harmless browning that happens to avocados when exposed to air, make this recipe shortly before serving and don't skip the lime juice.

NUT AND SEED OAT BARS

- MAKES 4 SERVINGS -

ALMONDS PAGE 107
OATS PAGE 89
CRANBERRIES PAGES 67, 68

These fiber-rich bars are perfect for satisfying your sweet tooth or providing an afternoon energy boost. Made with a base of rolled oats and speckled with almonds, pumpkin seeds, and dried cranberries, they're full of antioxidants, vitamin E, and fiber that nourish gut bacteria. Homemade bars are just as tasty as store-bought varieties, but you're able to control what ingredients you use. Feel free to modify the recipe to suit your needs and preferences.

INGREDIENTS

1 cup creamy almond butter
1/3 cup honey
1/2 teaspoon vanilla extract
2 cups rolled oats
1/2 teaspoon cinnamon
1/4 cup chopped almonds
1/4 cup pumpkin seeds
1/4 cup dried cranberries

Method

1. Fit a piece of parchment paper into an 8x8-in baking dish and set aside.

2. In a large bowl, whisk together the almond butter, honey, and vanilla. Add the oats, cinnamon, almonds, pumpkin seeds, and dried cranberries. Stir until well-mixed. Alternatively, you can combine all of the ingredients except the dried cranberries in a food processor. Pulse until combined, then stir in the cranberries.

3. Transfer the batter to the lined baking dish and press it into a single layer. Refrigerate for a few hours or overnight until the batter hardens. Slice into four bars, and enjoy.

EASY ALTERNATIVES

- Mix up the flavors by substituting chopped dried cherries or apricots in place of cranberries and pecans in place of almonds.
- Make this into energy balls instead of bars.
- For even more fiber and nutrients, add a tablespoon of milled flaxseed to the batter.
- To make these bars suitable for someone with nut allergies, replace the almond butter with sunflower seed butter and the chopped almonds with sunflower seeds.

STORAGE OPTIONS

Store the bars in an airtight container in the refrigerator for up to one week. To freeze them, place the bars on a plate and freeze for a couple of hours. Place in an airtight bag in the freezer for up to three months.

[INDEX]

[ACKNOWLEDGMENTS]

ABOUT THE AUTHOR

Lizzie Streit, MS, RDN, LD is a registered dietitian, nutrition writer, and recipe developer with a master's degree in human nutrition. She is the creator of It's a Veg World After All® and author of *The Complete Guide to Natural Vitamins* and *Vegetable Cookbook for Vegetarians: 200 Recipes from Artichoke to Zucchini*. Through her published works and recipes, she is devoted to helping others achieve and maintain good health by increasing their knowledge of nutrition and cooking skills. When she's not in the kitchen, Lizzie enjoys exploring the local food scene in Minneapolis, exercising around the lakes and trails, and experimenting with her backyard vegetable garden. To see more of her work, visit **itsavegworldafterall.com**.

PICTURE CREDITS

t = top; c = center; b = bottom; l = left; r = right

Shutterstock
Pages 4–5 Yuliya Gontar; 6 kina8; 7 DenisMArt; 8 Zu Kamilov; 10, 102 Natalia Lisovskaya; 11 Linda Hughes Photography; 14b, 28t Fascinadora; 16, 94, 138 Antonina Vlasova; 17 Natasha Breen; 18, 34, 40, 58, 66, 76, 92, 104, 112, 120, 128, 130 New Africa; 19 nelea33; 28b Maslova Valentina; 29 Sea Wave; 30 77 Studio; 31 Garmasheva Natalia; 32–33 5PH; 36 Irina Rostokina; 39t Nina Firsova; 39bl Lapina Maria; 39br Besedina Julia; 42 Melnikov Sergey; 44 Chursina Viktoriia; 46 natalia bulatova; 50 IriGri; 52 YARUNIV Studio; 54 barmalini; 56 MasterQ; 60 Lyudmila Zavyalova; 62 Foxys Forest Manufacture; 64 Valentina_G; 68 Sarka_Ab; 69t Xan; 69bl MARYIA SAMALEVICH; 69br, 136 Vladislav Noseek; 72, 78 virtu studio; 80 almaje; 82 badboydt7; 84 Jagoda Przybyla; 86 Olga_Rusinova; 88 Sasha Turkina; 90 Katarzyna Hurova; 97t Anna_Pustynnikova; 97b JeniFoto; 98, 143 1989studio; 100 Pinkasevich; 108 Tanya Sid; 110 pets and foods; 114 Oksana Mizina; 116 Netrun78; 118 Tacar; 122 Piece of Cake; 124 Marian Weyo; 126 Indian Food Images; 132 baibaz; 134 Africa Studio; 140–41 j.chizhe; 145 Elena Elizarova; 147, 151 Olga Nayashkova; 149 Losangela; 153 Ekaterina Kondratova; 155 rontav; 157 ManaswiPatil.

Unsplash
Pages 12 Bruno Nascimento; 13 Mariana Medvedeva; 14t Monika Grabkowska; 15 Rezel Apacionado; 21 Brooke Lark; 24 Tetiana Bykovets; 26 Ella Olsson; 27t Victoria Shes; 27b Shannon Milling; 48, 70 Kim Daniels; 74 Miguel Andrade

Dreamstime
Page 106 Baibaz

Allie Bornstein Photography
Page 160

All trademarks, trade names, and other product designations referred to herein are the property of their respective owners and are used solely for identification purposes. This book is a publication of The Bright Press, an imprint of The Quarto Group, and has not been authorized, licensed, approved, sponsored, or endorsed by any other person or entity. The publisher is not associated with any product, service, or vendor mentioned in this book. While every effort has been made to credit contributors, The Bright Press would like to apologize should there have been any omissions or errors, and would be pleased to make the appropriate correction for future editions.